THE SPACE-GODS REVEALED

The Space-Gods Revealed

A Close Look at the Theories of Erich von Däniken

RONALD STORY

NEW ENGLISH LIBRARY
TIMES MIRROR

To Rita

Grateful acknowledgement is made for permission to reprint the following material:

Excerpt on pages xiii and xiv from 'Pseudoscience' by P. H. Abelson, from *Science*, vol. 184, p. 1233, 21 June 1974 issue. Copyright 1974 by the American Association for the Advancement of Science.

Quotation on page v from the 11 June 1973 *Time* magazine essay, 'The Uncommonness of Common Sense' by Stephan Kanfer. Reprinted by permission from *Time*. Copyright Time Inc. 1973.

Excerpts on pages 88–90 appeared in German in *Der Spiegel*, No. 12/1973.

First published simultaneously in the United States of America by Harper and Row Publishers, Inc., and in Canada by Fitzhenry and Whiteside Ltd., Toronto.

First published in Great Britain by New English Library in 1976.

*

FIRST NEL PAPERBACK EDITION MAY 1978

*

NEL Books are published by
New English Library Limited from Barnard's Inn, Holborn, London EC1N 2JR.
Made and printed in Great Britain by Hunt Barnard Printing Ltd., Aylesbury, Bucks.

45003370 8

There are three kinds of senses: physical, common and non-. The first is used (and abused) by everyone. The last has become the property of infants, absurdists and politicians. And the one in the middle? Strung between the poles of the super-rational and the occult, it suffers from disuse and neglect. The nation suffers along with it.

— Stephan Kanfer in *Time* Magazine

Contents

Contents

ILLUSTRATIONS

Between pages 32 and 33

A rock carving of a head at Easter Island
The Piri Re'is map of 1513
Nazca lines and markings
The 'condor' on Nazca plain and the stars of the constellation Pavo,
    the Peacock, superimposed
Easter Island statues with topknots
Partly buried statues at the quarry at Rano Raraku, Easter Island
    and raising the statue at Anakena, Easter Island
Seven re-erected statues at Ahu a Kivi, an Easter Island ceremonial
    centre
The ruined Pyramid of Meidum and the Bent Pyramid of Dahshur

Between pages 128 and 129

Close-up photo of the stone carving of the Palenque 'astronaut'
The open sarcophagus with the remains of Pacal
Jabbaren, the 'great Martian god'
The rustproof iron pillar near Delhi, India
Map of Elephantine Island
An Egyptian mummy at the Cairo Museum
The Meridiani Sinus region of Mars photographed by *Mariner 9* and
    a section of Percival Lowell's map showing the Meridiani Sinus
    canal network
Close-up view of the Martian moon Phobos

Foreword

Lately I find myself giving a relatively large number of popular lectures on the possibility of extraterrestrial life, and it is a rare lecture after which I am not asked about the works of Erich von Däniken. His writings are very popular – although sometimes for peculiar reasons. I once overheard a couple discussing *Chariots of the Gods?* at a bookstand:

'Oh, don't you just love those Roman adventure stories?'

'But this one is kind of religious, I think.'

They then went off comparing *Chariots of the Gods?* unfavorably with the movie version of *Quo Vadis* and *The Robe*. While it was evident that neither had read von Däniken, the comparisons seemed appropriate.

Von Däniken's thesis is that a significant fraction of the monumental architecture, ancient artifacts, and some smaller works of graphic art of past ages were constructed not by humans but by benevolent beings from outer space. There is nothing *a priori* absurd in this contention; it is absurd only *a posteriori*. The possibility of extraterrestrial intelligence is something I and many other scientists take very seriously – to the point of using large radio telescopes to listen for possible signals sent our way by beings on planets of other stars. If there were good evidence that in the past we were visited by such beings, our task would be made immeasurably easier. But unfortunately there is no such evidence, as the present book helps to make clear. We must be very careful not to permit our hopes and wishes on such important questions to cloud our judgment. The ultimate arbiter is nature alone; and we must accept arguments for extraterrestrial visitations to earth only when the evidence is compelling.

Essentially, von Däniken's argument is that our ancestors were too stupid to create the most impressive surviving ancient architectural and artistic works. But people hundreds or thousands of years ago were in no significant way genetically different from people today. They had the same hopes and aspirations, organizational skills, and intellectual and artistic abilities. What is more, close inspections of von Däniken's books show a persistent suppression of the abundant archaeological evidence that these were the constructions of human beings. To take one example, there are inscriptions in ancient Egyptian hieroglyphics on individual massive stone blocks which constitute the great pyramids reading the rough equivalent of 'My goodness, we did it Tiger Team 11'. This seems an unlikely inscription by a group of interstellar spacefarers; but it is an extremely human response. Another Egyptian pyramid had its angle to the horizontal shallowed noticeably midway in the course of construction – because the original very steep angle of construction was discovered (too late) to be inconsistent with the strengths of materials. An identical pyramid, begun a little earlier, fell down. This architectural mistake in the two earliest pyramids is an unlikely one for a race of superhuman spacemen capable of traveling between the stars, but is very plausible for intelligent, enthusiastic, and inexperienced human monument builders.

I hope that one salutary consequence of books like *Chariots of the Gods?* will be a resurgence in the exciting field called archaeology, which covers, among other things, the study of how ancient monuments were in fact constructed. A fascinating introduction to this subject is contained in the book *The Ancient Engineers* by L. Sprague de

Camp. The present book by Ron Story among its other virtues provides a very pleasant excursion among some of the more interesting monuments and artifacts of ancient human civilizations. I also hope for the continuing popularity of books like *Chariots of the Gods?* in high school and college logic courses, as object lessons in sloppy thinking. I know of no recent books so riddled with logical and factual errors as the works of von Däniken. A careful reading of *Chariots of the Gods?* with the cheerful guidance of Ron Story and a dollop of reasonable skepticism can do a substantial amount of good in a society daily asked to believe contentions even more implausible than those of Erich von Däniken. We need practice in skepticism, as recent political events have so clearly demonstrated.

The popularity of von Däniken must, I think, be theological in origin. Our times are very perilous. The immediate relevance of traditional religions to contemporary problems is not so obvious as was once the case. At just this moment arises the beguiling doctrine that all-powerful, all-knowing, and benevolent creatures have in the past and will one day in the future come out of the sky and save us from ourselves.

Imitator publications, designed to trap the unwary von Däniken addict, are flourishing. The typography of the covers of many of these books is similar – large block letters in three dimensions casting shadows, the kind of type I associate with early *Superman* comics. The choice of typography is probably no accident. Von Däniken's thesis is a pop religion exactly on the intellectual level of *Superman* comics, but without *Superman*'s verve.

That writing as careless as von Däniken's, whose principal thesis is that our ancestors were dummies, should be so popular is a sober commentary on the credulousness and despair of our times. But the idea that beings from elsewhere will save us from ourselves is a very dangerous doctrine – akin to that of the quack doctor whose ministrations prevent the patient from seeing a physician competent to help him and perhaps to cure his disease. There are people of all ages who, having seen no reasoned critique of von Däniken's

11

doctrines, think that they must be true. As one rental car agent told me, 'If it wasn't true, they wouldn't let him print it,' But many publishers, I fear, are not so much interested in truth as in money. The times are such that simplistic doctrines like von Däniken's sell – even though they may represent, as I believe they do, a small but definite social danger.

Mr Story is to be commended for having performed the social service of writing in simple language a reasoned critique of some of the many errors in von Däniken's writings.

CARL SAGAN
*Professor of Astronomy and Space Sciences
and Director, Laboratory for Planetary Studies,
Cornell University*

Acknowledgments

I wish to express my appreciation to many professional people who kindly gave of their time to help me in various ways. The following persons (alphabetically listed) have contributed suggestions, advice, information, illustrations, and/or special writings for use in this book:

Frank D. Drake, Professor of Astronomy, and Director of the National Astronomy and Ionosphere Center, Cornel University

Robert S. Ellwood, Jr, Professor of Religion, University of Southern California

Edwin N. Ferdon, Jr, Associate Director of the Arizona State Museum, University of Arizona

Jeanne Flagg, Editor, Harper & Row, Publishers

Richard Greenwell, former Assistant Director of the Aerial Phenomena Research Organization(A.P.R.O.), currently Associate Editor for the Office of Arid Lands Studies, University of Arizona

William K. Hartmann, Senior Scientist of the Planetary Science Institute, Tucson, Arizona

Thor Heyerdahl, explorer, anthropologist, and author

J. Allen Hynek, Professor and Chairman, Department of Astronomy, and Director, Lindheimer Astronomical Research Center, Northwestern University

Stephen Larson, Research Assistant, Lunar and Planetary Laboratory, University of Arizona

William Mulloy, Professor of Anthropology, University of Wyoming

William L. Rathje, Associate Professor of Anthropology, University of Arizona

Merle Greene Robertson, archaelogical illustrator, Department of Pre-Columbian Art Research, Robert Louis Stevenson School, Pebble Beach, California

Carl Sagan, Professor of Astronomy and Space Sciences, and Director of the Laboratory of Planetary Studies, Cornell University

Joseph L. Scott, former Assistant Professor of German Pennsylvania State University, currently an educational consultant in Tucson, Arizona

Thomas L. Swihart, Professor of Astronomy, Steward Observatory, University of Arizona

Laird Thompson, astronomer, Kitt Peak National Observatory

Raymond E. White, Lecturer in Astronomy and Research Associate, Steward Observatory, University of Arizona

Preface

The ancient astronaut theory of Erich von Däniken proposes that beings from outer space came to earth in the distant past and created man in their image. This astounding idea represents a general assault on both academic science and many of the world's religions. However, most of our anthropologists, archaeologists, astronomers, theologians, and philosophers have remained silent on the issue.

The academic community has pretty much taken the attitude that the theory of ancient astronauts is beneath the dignity of serious investigators even to consider. The whole idea, they feel, is simply nonsense from the beginning. Why spend valuable professional time on a subject so obviously absurd when there are more important things to do?

As this book was being written, an editorial by Philip H. Abelson appeared in *Science* (the journal of the American Association for the Advancement of Science), part of which follows:

> During the last few years elements of the public and particularly of university students have turned increasingly to mysticism and to what I would call pseudoscience. The top sellers at campus bookstores have included such books as *Chariots of the Gods?*, *Gods from Outer Space*, . . . and others like them. . . .
> The popularity of pseudoscience books at universities should

be a source of concern to academic people, particularly scientists. The new trend comes at a time when many universities have abandoned requirements that students be exposed to as little as one science course. It is not pleasant to contemplate a situation in which our future leaders are being steeped in fantasy and are exposed to a putdown of science without effective response. The university community has a special obligation which it has not been meeting very well. It should move toward providing antidotes to the new intellectual poisons. In meeting these challenges to rationality, we should all remember that although humanity is eager to accept mysticism, it is also capable of yearning for truth.

But how do we find truth if no one will help us? The complacency of most academicians closes them off as a source of information. The high schools and elementary schools are doing little more than the colleges in combating the pseudosciences. Students are taught the steps of the scientific method and told to keep an open mind, but they are not given the critical tools and practice in using them that are necessary to evaluate a given theory. Few readers of books on the modern cults have the time or the inclination to check out the myriad 'facts' put forth to support them.

And so the pseudosciences go largely unexamined and continue to flourish. It is my hope that this book will provide an antidote to one pseudoscience – that popularized by Erich von Däniken.

1

The von Däniken Phenomenon

Few books have captured the imagination and appealed to the religious yearnings of the general public as much as *Chariots of the God's?* (1968), *Gods from Outer Space* (1968), and *The Gold of the Gods* (1973) by Erich von Däniken. The arrival of the 'ancient astronauts' has been heralded by two major network television specials, two 'major motion pictures', and more than sixty books that refer either directly or indirectly to von Däniken's theories. The American NBC-TV special 'In Search of Ancient Astronauts' gave the Swiss amateur archaeologist the boost he needed to attain super best-sellerdom (sales of more than 12 million copies in the United States, 34 million worldwide) and spawned what the Australian press has diagnosed as 'Dänikenitis'.

Von Däniken was born in Zofingen, Switzerland, on April 14, 1935. Raised as a strict Catholic, he attended the international Catholic school Saint-Michel, in Fribourg, Switzerland. At the age of nineteen he had an intense vision, the details of which he declines to discuss. He does claim to have obtained some of his information during periods of intense introspection and from experiences of *déjà vu*.[1]

After a communications breakdown over philosophical issues with his father and the Church, his formal education ended, and he became apprenticed to a Swiss hotelier. Starting as a cook and waiter, he worked his way up to manager. But life as a hotelier did not satisfy his philosophical and religious curiosities; he was much more interested in archaeology and astronomy and their relationship to religion. During his managership of the hotel Rosenhügel in Davos, von Däniken wrote his first book. He worked on it, so the story goes, after the guests had gone to bed, often until four in the morning.

The manuscript was accepted by Econ-Verlag in early 1967. The publisher then hired Wilhelm Roggersdorf, a screen writer and film producer who knew the public's tastes, to edit it. The work as published is said to have been extensively rewritten by Roggersdorf.[2]

In March 1968, Econ printed six thousand copies of *Erinnerungen an die Zukunft* ('Memories of the Future'). Two days after the first copies appeared, Swiss newspaper, *Weltwoche*, began a serialization, and additional printings of the book followed. The von Däniken movement spread from Switzerland to Germany, and by December 1968 the German edition of what would later be known to the English-speaking world as *Chariots of the Gods?* was the number-one-selling book in West Germany.

The first translation into English came in 1969 (published by Souvenir Press of London), and the first American hardcover edition appeared in 1970 (G. P. Putnam's Sons). The Bantam paperback edition was launched in February 1971, with a first printing of 207,200 copies. In the meantime, a German-made film version of *Chariots of the Gods?* had been produced by Terra Filmkunst of Berlin. After its success in Canada in the spring of 1972, the Americans became interested.

Alan Landsburg Productions (known for such famous television work as 'The Undersea World of Jacques Cousteau') took on the job of editing out about a third of the German film for a television special to be entitled 'In Search of Ancient Astronauts'. The show was first aired on NBC-TV on 5 January 1973. In the forty-eight hours that followed, Bantam Books sold more than a quarter of a million paperback copies of *Chariots* and the von Däniken controversy was well on its way. A few months later, the American distribution rights to the film *Chariots of the Gods?* were obtained by Sun International Productions, and the movie premiered in Buffalo, New York, on 14 November 1973. Landsburg, who took a cue from his earlier success with this theme, has since produced another television special, 'In Search of Ancient Mysteries', plus a full-length movie (released by Sun Classic Pictures) entitled *The Outer Space Connection*. Both films were followed by paperback books (written by Landsburg and his wife, Sally, and published by Bantam) bearing the same titles.

The actual writing of von Däniken's *Chariots of the Gods?* took place in 1966, the same year that the 'God is Dead' movement got under way. It was also the year of the publication of *Intelligent Life in the Universe*, a masterful work composed by astronomers I. S. Shklovskii of the U.S.S.R. and Carl Sagan of the U.S. This book contained many ideas that were later expressed (although some in a distorted form) in *Chariots*; it may well have given von Däniken the brainstorm to provide the world with a new set of gods to worship, to replace the traditional deity, who was being murdered by the poison pens of contemporary theologians.

Shklovskii and Sagan gave a certain legitimacy to the idea that extraterrestrial visits to earth may have taken place at various times before and after the advent of *Homo sapiens*. However, the examples given were clearly labeled as possibilities, and no claim was made that the earth was colonized by a crew of meddling cosmic gods.

Actually, this intriguing idea, complete with examples of alleged evidence – much of it identical with that cited by von Däniken – appeared in books published several years prior to the first edition of *Chariots of the Gods?*

The most notable of von Däniken's predecessors, to whom he gives very little credit, are the French authors Louis Pauwels, Jacques Bergier, and Robert Charroux. Pauwels and Bergier's *The Morning of the Magicians*,[3] published in France in 1960, contained references to electric batteries in the museum of Baghdad, mysteries of the Great Pyramid, Easter Island, Tiahuanaco, the Mayas, the plain of Nazca, and the Piri Re'is map. Charroux, whose *One Hundred Thousand Years of Man's Unknown History*[4] preceded von Däniken's first book by five years, discussed the Piri Re'is map, the Great Pyramid, the Ark of the Covenant as an electric condenser, the 'Candlestick of the Andes' (a large trident figure on a hill above the Bay of Pisco in Peru) as an ancient seismograph, the alleged atomic destruction of Sodom and Gomorrah (a speculation credited to M. M. Agrest), the Tassili 'Martian', and many other pieces of 'evidence' von Däniken cites.

These parallels came to the attention of Charroux's publisher shortly after von Däniken's *Erinnerungen an die Zukunft* appeared in Switzerland and Germany in March of 1968. As there was some talk of a possible suit for plagiarism, Econ-Verlag decided to include Charroux as a source in the bibliography of a later edition.[5] According to *Playboy* Magazine,[6] von Däniken has admitted that other writers proposed these theories based on the same evidence long before he did, and he says in the foreword to his second book, *Gods from Outer Space*, that he hoped 'questions of the kind that are *also* [italics mine] asked by Louis Pauwels, Jacques Bergier, and Robert Charroux will be answered in my lifetime'.[7] In the same book, von Däniken's editor, Roggersdorf, admits that 'von Däniken was not the first man who dared to challenge them' – i.e., previous explanations of the origin of the human race.[8]

However, von Däniken was not satisfied merely to read about the strange 'evidence' of ancient astronauts. During his managership of the Rosenhügel hotel he set out for Egypt, Lebanon, and North and South America to see things for himself. Unfortunately, the cost of such trips and his rising style of living far exceeded his income, and he soon found himself seriously in debt. In November 1968 he was arrested for fraud and two years later convicted of embezzlement, fraud, and forgery. He received a sentence of three and one-half years in prison and was fined 3,000 francs. (Ironically, by that time his book had been published and his debts paid out of the considerable royalties. He did not serve the full sentence.)

Von Däniken immediately entered a plea of nullity.° He defended the actions he was accused of – falsifying book-keeping entries and credit references in order to obtain loans – on the basis of lack of evil intentions. Credit instructions, he pointed out, are aware that potential clients may be poor risks and expect to be supplied misinformation; consequently, it is their responsibility to satisfy themselves of the financial situation of the borrower. The Court of Appeals rejected this interpretation. Von Däniken also complained that his sentence did not take into account his personality as an author. He held that a writer, in his eagerness to realize an idea that obsesses him, may sacrifice things, even moral values, he would otherwise hold dear. The court replied that the writer is certainly free to sacrifice things he would otherwise treasure, but only if he does not infringe on the rights of others.

In the next chapter we shall see how von Däniken the writer has similarly set himself above the laws of logic and scientific method. His readers, like credit institutions, must bear the responsibility of satisfying themselves of the validity of his claims and methods.

2

The Theory and the 'Proof'*

Although von Däniken admits he is 'not a scientific man',[1] he has not hesitated to adopt the terminology and methods of scientific investigation. 'Our historical past,' he explains in *Chariots of the Gods?*, 'is pieced together from indirect knowledge. Excavations, old texts, cave drawings, legends, and so forth were used to construct a working hypothesis ... If new aspects of [our historical past] turn up, the old working hypothesis, however familiar it may have become, must be replaced by a new one. It seems the moment has come to introduce a new working hypothesis and place it at the very center of our research into the past.'[2]

So far, so good. Let us see how well von Däniken has presented his hypothesis and provided evidence for it. But first we should be sure we know what is meant by scientific method. It began with the English statesman-philosopher Francis Bacon (1561–1626), who considered Aristotle's deductive logic unfruitful in the search for knowledge of the universe. One should not take for granted the truth of a generalization, he felt. Rather, one should try to verify it by continued observation and experimentation.

---

* In this chapter and most of those that follow, *Chariots of the Gods?* will be the book most often referred to because it is von Däniken's best-known work and the one that sets forth his hypothesis and introduces the main pieces of evidence offered in its support.

Scientific method as it has evolved from Bacon's ideas consists of the following steps:

1. Observing and gathering of facts.
2. Formulating a hypothesis, or generalization, that explains or accounts for these facts. A hypothesis should involve a minimum of assumptions and presuppositions, and it should be logically possible.
3. Testing or verifying the hypothesis. This involves the examination of any conclusions that can be deduced or predicted from it.
4. Determining the probable truth of the hypothesis if it has survived the testing process.

Von Däniken has certainly made observations, gathered 'facts', and formulated a hypothesis. Here it is, framed as a proclamation, from the introduction to *Chariots of the Gods?*

> I claim that our forefathers received visits from the universe in the remote past, even though I do not yet know who these extra-terrestrial intelligences were or from which planet they came. I nevertheless proclaim that these 'strangers' annihilated part of mankind existing at the time and produced a new, perhaps the first, *homo sapiens.*[3]

This hypothesis, while quite unlikely, is not logically or physically impossible; in fact, one underlying supposition – that intelligent life may exist elsewhere in the universe – is now denied by practically no one who is reasonably well informed on the subject. It is interesting to recall here Bertrand Russell's example of an improbable yet logically irrefutable hypothesis:

> Opponents of Darwin, such as Edmund Gosse's father [Philip Gosse], urged [this] argument against evolution. The world, they said, was created in 4004 B.C., complete with fossils, which were inserted to try our faith. The world was created suddenly, but was made such as it would have been if it had evolved. There is no logical impossibility about this view. And similarly there is no logical impossibility in the view that the world was created five minutes ago, complete with memories and records. This may

seem an improbable hypothesis, but it is not logically refutable.[4]

After stating his 'revolutionary' hypothesis, von Däniken tells us he is going to try to provide evidence for it. However, he is well aware that he cannot really prove his assertion. In discussing ancient legends, he admits this quite clearly:

> When arguing about the entirely new aspects that I introduce into investigation of the past, the objection might be made that it is not possible to complete everything in the ancient traditions that points to heavenly apparitions into a sequence of proofs of prehistoric space travel. But that is not what I am doing. I am simply referring to passages in very ancient texts that have no place in the working hypothesis in use up to the present.[5]

Von Däniken does not have any qualms, however, about building up an elaborate scenario, as we may call it, for the 'new Genesis' of man that would somehow provide evidence for his theory. He tells of a hypothetical spaceship that happened to discover earth. The alien visitors were not long in noticing that our planet had the necessary conditions for the development of intelligent life, and so, to speed up the process, they began breeding experiments on the apelike creatures ('no *Homo sapiens* but something rather different') they found there. They 'artificially fertilized' some of the females. Thousands of years later the spacemen returned and found 'scattered specimens' of *Homo sapiens.* Fearing that these barbarians might retrogress to their former habit of mating with animals, the genetic engineers 'wiped out the freaks' or resettled them on other worlds. The successful specimens that remained were now intelligent enough to learn the basics of civilization. Hence, 'the first communities and the first skills came into being; rock faces and cave walls were painted, pottery was discovered, and the first attempts at architecture were made'.[6]

Because the visitors came from a place unknown, the primitive earth-men considered them as 'gods' and had great respect for them. The spacemen watched over the earth creatures as gods should and made sure that they did not fall into evil ways.

Anticipating the reader's reaction to this audacity, von Däniken hastens to say:

> Admittedly this speculation is still full of holes. I shall be told that proofs are lacking. The future will show how many of those holes can be filled in. This book puts forward a hypothesis made up of many speculations, therefore the hypothesis must not be 'true'. Yet when I compare it with the theories enabling many religions to live unassailed in the shelter of their taboos, I should like to attribute a minimal percentage of probability to my hypothesis. [7]

But the above account of man's origin is not von Däniken's only scenario. In *The Gold of the Gods*[8] he offers quite a different one to account for the gigantic system of tunnels he claims exists in Ecuador and Peru. In this scenario, the founders of humanity were 'losers' in a cosmic war. Fleeing their enemies in a spaceship, they spotted the planet earth. Earth's atmosphere was far from ideal for them. However, they landed and built a series of underground tunnels to provide a temporary refuge from their pursuers. As a decoy, they set up 'technical stations and transmitters' on what was then the fifth planet of the solar system. The enemy spacemen, as expected, annihilated the decoy planet, the remains of which now make up the asteroid belt between the orbits of Mars and Jupiter. They then departed, thinking they had destroyed the losers.

The losers' problems were not over yet. With the explosion, the axis of the earth shifted, causing the great flood recounted in legends from around the world. After riding out the flood, the losers ventured out onto the surface of the earth. They had to wear 'gas masks' until they became accustomed to the terrestrial atmosphere; this is why we find cave drawings of helmets and breathing equipment.

They then turned their attention to the 'monkeys' that were already in existence at the time. By manipulating their genes, they created intelligent beings in their own image. But the losers, now gods, grew impatient with the progress of these early humans and were 'quick to punish and wipe out the malcontents'. The losers became the bad guys. To escape their wrath, the people dug underground hideouts, which can still be seen in many parts of the world.

Von Däniken's speculations are not confined to these scenarios. Throughout the book in presenting his 'evidence' from ancient monuments, artifacts, and texts, he calls upon his fertile imagination. 'Let us imagine for a moment,' he tells us, 'that Sodom and Gomorrah were destroyed . . . by a nuclear explosion. Perhaps – let us speculate a little further – the "angels" simply wanted to destroy some dangerous fissionable material and at the same time to make sure of wiping out a human brood they found unpleasant.'[9] After remarking on the sudden departure of the Mayas from their cities, he invites us to 'pretend that this event, this enormous national migration, happened in ancient Egypt'.[10] This passage also illustrates Von Däniken's fondness for arguing by analogy.

In the following passage, von Däniken eases us smoothly into his fantasy with a series of assumptions:

> *Let us suppose* that foreign astronauts visited the territory of the Sumerians thousands of years ago. *Let us assume* that they laid the foundations of the civilization and culture of the Sumerians and then returned to their own planet, after giving this stimulus to development. *Let us postulate* that curiosity drove them back to the scene of their pioneer work every hundred terrestrial years to check the results of their experiment. By the standards of our present-day expectation of life the same astronauts *could easily* have survived for 500 terrestrial years.[11] [Italics added.]

At one point in *Chariots of the Gods?*, von Däniken assures us that he is not letting his imagination go too far. Discussing a being in a well painting in Tassili, in the Sahara, he says, 'Without overstretching my imagination, I got the impression that the great God Mars is depicted in a space or diving suit.'[12]

A favorite device of von Däniken's is the rhetorical question. He urges us to 'take another look at the forest of question marks [which he himself has created] – the array of unexplained mysteries. Do they make sense as the remains of prehistoric space travelers?[13] In the following passage he tries to force a conclusion on us by a battery of rhetorical questions:

> Is it all mere coincidence? Are they all merely individual fancies, strange whims on the part of our ancestors? Or is there an ancient promise of corporeal return that is unknown to us? Who could have made it?[14]

And again:

> But what if the frescoes, at Tassili or in the United States or in France, actually reproduce what the primitive peoples saw? What should we say if the spirals on the rods really depicted antennae, just as the primitive peoples have seen them on the unfamiliar gods? Isn't it possible that things which ought not to exist do in fact exist?[15]

Von Däniken sometimes puts us off guard by admitting that one of his theories is pure speculation, and then goes on to make a daring jump to a conclusion. After stating that 'It is not yet possible to say with certainty whether the plain of Nazca was ever an airfield,' he asserts that 'Enormous drawings that were undoubtedly meant as signals for a being floating in the air are found on mountainsides in many parts of Peru,' clinching his argument with the ever-present rhetorical question: 'What other purpose could they have served?'[16]

Another daring jump to a conclusion comes in his discussion of the Ark of the Covenant. 'Undoubtedly the Ark was electrically charged!' he exclaims. As part of his 'evidence' for this assertion he searches his memory: 'Without actually consulting Exodus, I seem to remember that the Ark was often surrounded by flashing sparks and that Moses made use of this "transmitter" whenever he needed help and advice.'[17]

Non-sequiturs are everywhere. Von Däniken himself gives an example of this form of false argument wherein the conclusion does not follow from the premises. While mocking scientists of five hundred years ago, he quotes one of them as stating, 'Nowhere in the Bible . . . does it say that the earth revolves around the sun. Consequently every such assertion is the work of the devil!'[18] Then, a few pages later, he uses this form of reasoning to try to establish one of his own conclusions: ' "Giants" haunt the pages of almost all ancient books. So they must have existed.'[19]

Von Däniken's method of scientific investigation, as we have seen, rests heavily on elaborate scenarios and suppositions, flights of imagination, bombardments of rhetorical questions, and daring leaps to conclusions. His 'evidence' – archaeological and mythological – is a collection of interesting objects and ideas superficially described and taken out of context. Archaeologists view each artifact they unearth in relation to all others excavated with it or at other sites of similar or different age. Students of mythology interpret a particular myth in relation to myths from other lands and peoples. Both keep in mind what is known about the cultures and environments from which the subjects of their study came.

But perhaps the most serious deficiency in von Däniken's argument is his omission of so much relevant data that would cast an entirely different light on the subject at hand. Many examples of this will be found in later chapters. 'It's true,' he admits in an interview for *Playboy*, 'that I accept what I like and reject what I don't like, but every theologian does the same.' 'Except,' replied the interviewer, 'that you claim to be offering science, not theology . . .'[20]

Scientists, of course, have not always been right. They can be biased and resistant to new ideas, and their mistaken observations can lead to faulty theories. For example, the development of maggots in decomposed meat gave the illusion of life originating in front of one's very eyes and was accepted by scientists of the seventeenth and eighteenth centuries as evidence for the theory of spontaneous generation. Experiments beginning with those of Francesco Redi in 1668 and ending with those of Louis Pasteur in 1864 disproved the theory that life could arise from nonlife. 'Piltdown Man', a fossil skull put together from fragments found in England in 1912, was believed at the time to be the long-sought 'missing link' between ape and man. The delusion was ended in 1953 when the skull was subjected to fluorine dating tests that showed the bones to be modern – the jaw from an ape and the skull from a recent human.

Errors like these are eventually discovered by further testing and experimentation. This self-correcting feature of the scientific method is what makes it the valuable tool it is in our search for the truth.

3

Ancient Astronauts
and the Bible

The first serious suggestion that ancient astronauts may have visited the earth in Biblical times was made in 1956 by the American astrophysicist Morris K. Jessup in a book called *U.F.O. and the Bible.* 'Much of the past skepticism regarding the validity of the Bible,' he acknowledged, 'has sprung from the improbability of the events and forecasts recorded therein. The existence of space-intelligence . . . and the probability of a super-race using navigable contrivances, fits all conditions which we have been able to attribute to U.F.O.[s], and thus rationalizes scriptural events.'[1]

In 1959 another scientist, the Russian ethnologist M. M. Agrest, proposed a direct connection between some events described in the Bible and visitations by extraterrestrials. These ideas were taken up and elaborated upon in 1960 by UFOlogist Brinsley Le Poer Trench in his book *The Sky People.*[2] Trench, who has been called 'the evangelist and top theologian of what amounts to a new galactic religion',[3] claimed that the Hebrew version of the Old Testament refers to the Sky People when it uses the word *Elohim*, which is a plural form translated as 'God' in the English Bible. He, and von Däniken after him, called attention to certain passages in the English version of the Bible that retain the plural form, particularly Gen. 1:26: 'And God said, Let us make man in our image, after our likeness . . . ' 'Why does God speak in the plural?' asks von Däniken. ' . . . One would think that the one and only God ought to address mankind in the singular, not in the plural.'[4]

According to *The Oxford Annotated Bible*, 'The plural *us, our*, . . . probably refers to the divine beings who surround God in his heavenly court . . . and in whose *image* man was made.'[5] *The Interpreter's Bible* allows that 'Hebrew religious thought was familiar with the idea of a heavenly host with whom God took counsel'[6] but says that '*us* could indeed be taken simply as a plural of majesty, for the custom of rulers speaking in the plural appeared with the Persians . . . '[7]* Whatever the explanation, the passage in question hardly indicates a landing party of spacemen.

Continuing to pursue the idea of a plural God, von Däniken quotes again from Genesis (6:4): 'There were giants in the earth in those days; and also after that, when the sons of God came in unto the daughters of men, and they bare children to them, the same became mighty men which were of old, men of renown.' This is a difficult passage to interpret, but von Däniken seems to have no doubt as to its meaning: 'The Bible speaks of "giants" and describes them as "sons of God", and these "sons of God" breed with the daughters of men and multiply.'[8]

Who were these giants and 'sons of God'? According to *The Oxford Annotated Bible*, the sons of God were divine beings who belonged to the heavenly court.[9] But the 'giants' were not the 'sons of God', as von Däniken suggests. The Hebrew term translated as 'giants' in the King James Version of the Bible is *Nephilim*. *The Oxford Annotated Bible* identifies the *Nephilim* as 'men of gigantic stature whose super-

---

* It is interesting to read in *The Interpreter's Bible* (1:448) that the word *Elohim* is used instead of *Yahweh* in only the first of the two originally separate documents that made up the narrative of Genesis, and then only up to the time when God reveals his divine name, *Yahweh*, to Moses. The term seems to have had a supernatural connotation in the Canaanite culture, the precursor of Judaism. George B. Vetter tells us in his book *Magic and Religion* (New York: Philosophical Library, 1958, 1963, p. 36) that 'El . . . (plural *elim* or *elohim*) were personifications of the power believed to dwell in an object or phenomenon which excited awe in man. . . . Thus majestic mountains were "mountains of *el*", tall trees were "trees of *el*", mighty winds were the "breath of *elohim*".'

Was this head, carved on a rock at Easter Island, a self-portrait of a visitor from outer space? This question is raised in the film *Chariots of the Gods?*, commentary for which was written by Wilhelm Roggersdorf, editor of the German edition of *Chariots*. From the film *Chariots of the Gods? By permission of Sun Classic Pictures, Inc.*

The Piri Re'is map of 1513. Africa is at upper right (see elephant), South America is at lower left, and the southernmost part supposedly represents the bays and islands of the Antarctic coast now under an icecap. *From the map collection of the University of Arizona Library.*

Above: View down a typical Nazca line. Tire tracks exemplify damage being done by vehicles of local and foreign tourists. *Photo by William and Gayle Hartmann*

Left: Aerial view of Nazca markings. Meandering dry river channels cross area. Note damage from tire tracks in foreground. *Photo by William and Gayle Hartmann*

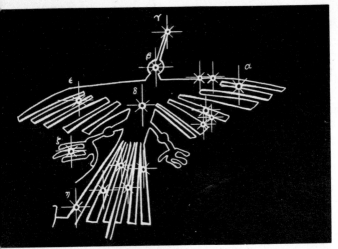

Above: Stars making up the southern-sky constellation Pavo, the Peacock, superimposed on the outline of a giant bird, identified as a condor, depicted on the Nazca plain. The drawing of the bird figure was adapted from an aerial photograph by Gerald S. Hawkins from *Beyond Stonehenge. Copyright © 1973 by Gerald S. Hawkins. By permission of Harper & Row, Publishers and Hutchinson Publishing Group Ltd.*

Below: Aerial photograph of condor on Nazca plain. The line running parallel to the wings is a solstice line. *Copyright © 1973 by Gerald S. Hawkins. By permission of Harper & Row, Publishers and Hutchinson Publishing Group Ltd.*

Easter Island statues with topknots, as they appeared to the first European visitors in the eighteenth century

Left: Exterior slope of the quarry at Rano Raraku, showing partly buried statues where they were originally left to await transportation to *ahu* platforms. The indigenous social order collapsed and civil war broke out, putting to an end ceremonial construction decades before the island was discovered by Europeans. *Reprinted with permission from Américas, monthly magazine published by the General Secretariat of the Organization of American States. Photo by William Mulloy*

Bottom left: Raising of the statue at Anakena. Statue is gradually lifted by levering building up a supporting mound of stones in alternating stages. *Photo courtesy of Thor Heyerdahl*

Below: Seven re-erected stone giants stand on the central platform of Ahu a Kivi, an Easter Island ceremonial centre that was restored in 1960. This is a relatively late *ahu*. Carbon-14 dating reveals its construction took place around A.D. 1500. *Reprinted by permission from Américas, monthly magazine published by the General Secretariat of the Organization of American States. Photo by William Mulloy*

Above: The ruined Pyramid of Meidum (c. 2630 B.C.) is surrounded by enormous mounds of rubble formed after the collapse of the original structure. *Drawing from History of Ancient Egypt, vol. 1, by George Rawlinson (New York; John W. Lovell Co., 1880)*

Below: The Bent Pyramid of Dahshur (c. 2600 B.C.). The abrupt change in the angle of slope from 54 to 42 degrees has been thought to be due to an alteration in design made to avoid a catastrophe like the one that befell the Pyramid of Meidum. *Drawing from History of Ancient Egypt, vol. 1, by George Rawlinson (New York: John W. Lovell Co., 1880)*

human power was thought to result from divine-human marriage' and the 'sons of God' as 'divine beings who belonged to the heavenly court'.[10] *The Interpreter's Bible* tells us that 'The beliefs that among the early inhabitants of the earth were men of great stature and that marriages of the gods with mortals frequently occurred are found in other ancient literatures.'[11] Thus von Däniken's idea that Martian giants came to earth and bred with man-apes gets little support from the Book of Genesis.

The destruction of Sodom and Gomorrah, von Däniken tells us, could have been caused by a nuclear explosion. The angels' urgency in getting Lot and his family away from the cities would then be explained by the fact that a countdown was in progress. However, the Biblical account does not suggest a nuclear explosion. Nuclear explosions are characterized by the rising of a dazzling ball of fire and a mushroom-shaped cloud, followed by a roll of thunder. In the passages from Genesis, fire and brimstone rained *down* on the cities, although smoke from the country did rise 'as the smoke of a furnace' (Gen. 19:28).

Von Däniken's interpretation of the story is somewhat startling: 'Those who were to escape it – such as the Lot family – had to stay a few miles from the center of the explosion in the mountains, for the rock faces would naturally absorb the powerful dangerous rays. And – we all know the story – Lot's wife turned around and looked straight at the atomic sun.'[12]

True enough, the Dead Sea (which is also called the Salt Sea) is a strange place. The ancient Greeks and Arabs handed down stories about poisonous gases arising out of the water, gases so lethal that birds attempting to fly over it would fall dead into the water before reaching the opposite shore.

When the first scientific investigators went into the area, in 1848, they observed that 'the air was filled with sharp acrid odors, a mixture of petroleum and sulphur', and that 'huge deposits of coagulated salt made the beach and the rock face above it sparkle in the sun like diamonds'.[13] They found

3

that, in contrast to the average 4.6 percent salt content of normal ocean waters, the Dead Sea is about 25 percent salt. No one can drown in the Dead Sea; people who go into the water float like corks. The high salt content has helped preserve the remnants of an ancient forest, which can be seen on the sea bottom in certain shallow areas. Conditions in this region were apparently quite different in earlier times.

Evidence indicates that the cataclysm described in the Bible did take place (probably around 2000 B.C.), as the result of a great earthquake accompanied by explosions of natural gas.

The ancient cities of Sodom and Gomorrah were located in the Great Rift Valley, which runs from a point several hundred miles north of Palestine, through the south shore of the Dead Sea, extending southward beyond the Red Sea into Africa. 'From time immemorial the area beyond this depression has been subject to earthquakes,' writes Werner Keller in *The Bible as History*.[14] Excavations have been made in the region of Sodom. According to Robert T. Boyd, an excavation in 1928 ' . . . revealed a stratum of salt 150 feet thick. Over this were large quantities of sulphur, or brimstone. The place was a burned out region of oil and asphalt, where a great rupture in the strata took place centuries ago.'[15]

An explanation exists, as well, for the story that Lot's wife turned into a pillar of salt. Near the southern shore of the Dead Sea there is a range of hills (called Jebel Usdum by the Arabs) composed principally of rock salt. Many large blocks of salt have been dislodged from their original positions by the rain, and have slid downhill. Some of them have curious shapes, which combined with their white color makes them look like carved statues. One such 'statue' has even been given the name 'Lot's Wife'.

Von Däniken's treatment of Ezekiel is interesting because of what he *doesn't* quote from the Bible as well as because of what he *does*. In *Chariots of the Gods?* he gives verse 1:1 as follows: 'Now it came to pass in the thirtieth year, in the fourth month, in the fifth day of the month, as I was among the captives by the river of Chebar, that the heavens were opened . . ."[16] What is left out is: ' . . . and I saw visions of God.' This makes quite a difference. Visions are not to be taken as literal descriptions; moreover, the subject of the vision is clearly identified as God. Von Däniken continues to quote as follows:

> And I looked, and, behold, a whirlwind came out of the north, a great cloud, and a fire infolding itself, and a brightness was about it, and out of the midst thereof as the color of amber, out of the midst of the fire. Also out of the midst thereof came the likeness of four living creatures. And this was their appearance; they had the likeness of a man. And every one had four faces, and every one had four wings. And their feet were straight feet; and the sole of their feet was like the sole of a calf's foot: and they sparkled like the color of burnished brass. (Ezek. 1:4–7.)

In other words, there appeared four *cherubims*. A cherub was a winged figure with a human head and an animal body, or as *Peloubet's Bible Dictionary* has it: 'a composite creature-form which finds a parallel in the religious insignia of Assyria, Egypt and Persia, e.g., the sphinx, the winged bulls and lions of Nineveh, etc."[17] These figures may originally have had an astronomical significance, as pointed out by C. P. S. Menon in *Early Astronomy and Cosmology*:

> . . . these are the constellations associated with the solstices and the equinoxes, the Lion of the summer solstice, and Bull of the vernal equinox, the Eagle, the early constellation that furnished the *Nakshatras* of the winter quarter, and perhaps the Babylonian Scorpion-man of the autumnal equinox; in the Apocalypse of St. John, the cherubs are called 'living creatures' – no doubt, of the Zodiac. Similar constellations guarding the four quarters have been shown to exist in other ancient countries.[18]

Von Däniken skips a few verses that give more details about the living creatures, including the fact that each had the face of a lion, an ox, and an eagle, and goes on to describe the wheels of the 'vehicle'.

> Now as I beheld the living creatures, behold one wheel upon the earth by the living creatures, with his four faces. The appear-

ance of the wheels and their work was like unto the color of a beryl: and they four had one likeness: and their appearance and their work was as it were a wheel in the middle of a wheel. When they went they went upon their four sides: and they turned not when they went. As for their rings, they were so high that they were dreadful; and their rings were full of eyes round about them four. And when the living creatures went, the wheels went by them: and when the living creatures were lifted up from the earth, the wheels were lifted up. (Ezek. 1:15-19.)

A helicopter, of course! Then von Däniken tells us of the voice that spoke to Ezekiel:

Son of man, stand upon thy feet, and I will speak unto thee. (Ezek. 2:1.)

... and I heard behind me a voice of a great rushing, saying, Blessed be the glory of the Lord from his place. I heard also the noise of the wings of the living creatures that touched one another, and the noise of the wheels over against them, and a noise of a great rushing. (Ezek. 3:12-13.)

'Who spoke to Ezekiel?' von Däniken asks. 'What sort of beings were they? They were certainly not "gods" in the traditional sense of the word, or they would not have needed a vehicle to move from one place to another.'[19] However, von Däniken did not quote the passage telling of the firmament over the heads of the cherubim and the 'likeness of the throne' above that, on which God sat in human form, just as he omitted the earlier phrase that Ezekiel's vision was of God.

Josef Blumrich, while he was chief of the systems layout branch at the Marshall Spaceflight Center of NASA, wrote a book entitled *The Spaceships of Ezekiel*, which can only be described as an extreme form of rationalization, with a good supply of technical jargon and diagrams. The space engineer believes, like von Däniken, that Ezekiel's visions were of a kind of helicopter. Verse by verse he analyzes Ezekiel's description of the components of the vehicle 'in the light of today's knowledge of spacecraft and rocket technology'.[20] He finds them 'amazingly accurate', making it possible for him (Blumrich) 'not only to develop a simple sketch, but also to express dimensions, weights, and capabilities in figures. Thus, for the first time, it became possible to free an ancient report on spaceships from its disguising pictures and to transpose it into the language of engineers.'[21]

The 'wheel in the middle of a wheel' was easy for the co-builder of Saturn V; he explains it in terms of a support and drive mechanism of the wheel segments. The 'eyes' on the rims were simply protrusions to keep the wheels from sliding on the ground. Blumrich obtained a patent on such a wheel design in 1974.

No Biblical passage was too diffcult for Blumrich to interpret, not even the one von Däniken failed to quote describing the four 'faces' of the 'living creatures'. The 'living creatures', of course, are the four helicopters that make up the vehicle. 'And we know from the technical description of the spaceship,' he explains, 'the gears and control mechanisms located immediately above the rotor plane are protected by a fairing. The latter has an irregular shape and is provided with protrusions and cutouts. Such a combination of structural features can assume a certain resemblance to faces or can best be described by such a comparison.'[22] Blumrich the engineer then allows himself a von Däniken-style speculation: ' . . . it is entirely thinkable that these beings at that time did what our pilots so often do today: paint or otherwise depict faces, birds, and so on, on the nose or sides of the fuselages of their aircraft just for fun.'[23] Von Däniken is, of course, delighted that 'an outstanding technician has taken my speculations with all the attendant evidence literally'.[24] That Blumrich has done so shows the fascination *Chariots of the Gods?* holds for our technologically oriented society.

Donald Menzel, a Harvard astronomer who has written extensively on U.F.O.s, suggests a meteorological basis for Ezekiel's 'wheels' and 'faces'. He refers to a rare phenomenon called 'parhelia', an 'optical effect caused by the passage of sunlight through a thin layer of ice crystals, usually associated with cirrus clouds'. The apparition takes the form of a ring of light around the sun, or sometimes *two* rings. Menzel explains as follows:

> A vertical and a horizontal streak of light may cross both rings like the spokes of a wheel. Indeed here is a reasonable and simple explanation for the 'wheel in the middle of a wheel' that Ezekiel saw. Although the two wheels are singularly devoid of color, except for a tinge of amber on the inner edge of the smaller wheel, an inverted bow colored like the rainbow with sapphire at the top extends above the outer wheel. The overall effect of this rare, complete parhelic display is that of a huge chariot, with one difference, as Ezekiel himself noted. As the wheels 'were lifted up from the earth' (following the rising sun), 'they turned not when they went.'[25]

He goes on to account for the 'faces':

> In the early days it was customary to carve the spokes of a wheel to the form of various creatures. It is, therefore, not surprising that Ezekiel visualized living forms in the four bright sundog condensations of the inner ring. The white feathery clouds of the spokes and also of the inner ring suggested wings, two covering the body and two outstretched. The eight outstretched wings of the four creatures formed the inner wheel.[26]

It is interesting to note that Menzel pointed out in 1953, three years before Jessup, that flying saucers were mentioned in the Bible, calling special attention to Ezekiel. However, he did not take Ezekiel's vision literally, nor did he suggest that Ezekiel was visited by ancient astronauts.

Theologians have also been known to succumb to 'flying sauceritis'. In the same year that *Chariots of the Gods?* was published in Germany (1968), a book, little known at the time, was published in the United States, entitled *The Bible and Flying Saucers*.[27] This piece of writing is particularly interesting, since the author, Barry H. Downing, is a pastor of the Northminster Presbyterian Church in Endwell, New York, and has qualifications greatly exceeding those of von Däniken for composing such a work. Downing received his B.A. degree from Hartwick College, where he majored in physics, and a B.D. degree from the University of Edinburgh, where he specialized in the comparative study of science and religion.

Downing's primary concern is the Book of Exodus. Interestingly enough, some of his interpretations are carryovers from Jessup and Trench. Take, for example, verse 3:2: 'And the angel of the Lord appeared unto him [Moses] in a flame of fire out of the midst of a bush: and he looked, and, behold, the bush burned with fire, and the bush was not consumed.' According to Jessup, Trench, and Downing, this passage denotes the presence of a U.F.O. Trench says, 'A spaceship – flying saucer – often illuminates the neighboring countryside with its electric forcefield. [When was this method of U.F.O. propulsion established?] The glowing light within this forcefield surrounding the ship would most certainly have caused the bush to look as if it was [*sic*] on fire.'[28] And in Downing's words, 'The U.F.O. in the thicket made the whole clump of bushes appear to be on fire, but apparently the thicket was not consumed by the presence of the U.F.O., and this combination of circumstances caught Moses' attention.'[29] The angel of the Lord, which apparently represented God, is conveniently forgotten in these interpretations.

Menzel, the astronomer, sees another rare natural phenomenon in the burning bush incident. Lightning can sometimes be discharged upward, giving branches of a tree or the rigging of a ship the appearance of being on fire.

Another example from Exodus in which Trench and Downing find a U.F.O. is in verses 13:21–22: 'And the Lord went before them by day in a pillar of a cloud, to lead them the way; and by night in a pillar of fire, to give them light; to go by day and night. He took not away the pillar of the cloud by day, nor the pillar of fire by night, from before the people.'

According to Trench, 'This is a wonderful description of a modern flying saucer.'[30] Downing agrees that the description is of a U.F.O., but does admit that the shape is not established definitely as a saucer.[31]

Because the pillar of cloud and the pillar of fire appeared

in the direction of Mount Sinai, I thought it might be helpful to look ahead at the Biblical passages that tell what occurred after the arrival of the Hebrews at their destination.

> And it came to pass on the third day in the morning, that there were thunders and lightnings, and a thick cloud upon the mount, and the voice of the trumpet exceeding loud . . . (19:16.)
>
> And mount Sinai was altogether on a smoke, because the Lord descended upon it in fire: and the smoke thereof ascended as the smoke of a furnace, and the whole mount quaked greatly. (19:18.)

This does suggest the pillar of cloud and the pillar of fire that the Hebrews were following; it is also a good description of a volcano, which can be seen at a great distance. Whether these phenomena were metaphors to convey the majesty of God or references to volcanic activity on Mount Sinai, we really don't know. But certainly the words 'pillar of smoke' and 'pillar of fire' are far more descriptive of a volcano than of a flying saucer.

The Bible, von Däniken tells us, is full of contradictions. So are his interpretations and those of other ancient astronaut believers.

4

A Genetic Miracle

In *Gods from Outer Space*, von Däniken tells why he thinks we should hear his theory:

> Certainly the track of racial development from hominids to *Homo sapiens* can be followed back clearly for millions of years, but we cannot make nearly so definite a statement about the *origin of intelligence*. There are minimal indications from the remote past, but they do not add up to a whole. So far I have not been fortunate enough to hear an explanation of the origin of intelligence in man that is even tolerably convincing.[1]

In other words, the human race became smart too fast. He goes on to ask: 'Is there a plausible explanation of why savages suddenly clothed themselves? . . . Who taught the savages to take the seeds of certain wild plants, pound them up, add water, and bake an article of food from the resulting mush? Why anthropoids, hominids and primitive men learned nothing for millions of years and then suddenly primitive men learned so much is a question that nags at me.'[2]

But the answer is soon forthcoming: Mankind is the creation of the astronaut-gods. In *Chariots of the Gods?* von Däniken was satisfied with the thesis that there was deliberate 'breeding' by giants who were 'sons of god' or escapees from Mars. This took place by sexual intercourse or by artificial fertilization, depending on which passage you read. By the time he got around to *Gods from Outer Space*, he had discovered D.N.A. and the genetic code and claimed that the breeding took place by 'artificial mutation of primitive man's genetic code by unknown intelligences. In that way,' he explained, 'the new men would have received their faculties suddenly – consciousness, memory, intelligence, a feeling for handicrafts and technology.'[3] Before the space-gods happened along, primitive man must have been a real zombie, stumbling about without even consciousness or memory!

Sometimes it is difficult to figure out what von Däniken has in mind. He has given us three different mechanisms for man's creation: (1) sexual intercourse, (2) artificial fertilization, and (3) artificial mutation through manipulation of the genetic code. In order for him to suggest any one of these means, his knowledge of biology and genetics would have to be extremely limited.

He seems to be unaware of the extreme unlikelihood of interfertility between the man-ape species and whatever species the space-gods might have been. His suggestion that the space-gods were *giants*, and that these giants had sexual intercourse with early man-apes at around 40,000 B.C., poses several major difficulties. To begin with, 40,000 B.C. was *at least a million years later* than the period during which these man-apes are known to have inhabited the African continent. (Incidentally, no such remains have yet been found in Tiahuanaco, Bolivia, von Däniken's chosen Garden of Eden.) And the hominids that did exist around 40,000 B.C. were rather small, averaging about five feet in height.

I will not elaborate on the problems this kind of limitation might impose on the mating process. Besides the unlikelihood that the physical form of von Däniken's interplanetary visitors would allow such a mating, a similarity in genetic make-up, which would be a biological necessity, even for artificial insemination, is unlikely in the extreme. Not only would the chromosomes of the two species have to be of the same shape and number, but their genes would have to be in the same basic arrangement and be located on corresponding chromosomes. This poses yet another flaw in the theory: if the chromosome number and the arrangement of genes on the chromosomes are similar enough to allow fertilization and viable offspring, the two beings would already be of the same or closely related species.

As is his way, von Däniken dismisses a troublesome problem with a rhetorical question. Acknowledging that a cross between man and animals is considered impossible, he asks, 'But do we know the genetic code according to which the chromosome count of the mixed beings was put together?" Here he really betrays his ignorance of genetics. The genetic code has no direct bearing on chromosome count; it codes genetic information by which proteins are synthesized in the cell.

Von Däniken's superficial understanding of modern genetics is further revealed by his misuse of the terminology. When scientists perform genetic surgery, or genetic engineering, which is what von Däniken's space-gods apparently undertook, they do not manipulate the *genetic code*, but manipulate the D.N.A., or deoxyribonucleic acid, which is the chemical name for the basic genetic material.

There is simply no reason to suspect what von Däniken calls an artificial mutation, or tinkering of any kind in the evolution of man. And even if there were, a classic philosophical problem would arise. If the astronaut-gods are necessary in explaining the origin of human intelligence, then other gods would be necessary to explain the origin of *their* intelligence, and so on, ad infinitum. Therefore this explanation renders the astronaut-gods superfluous.

There were significant changes, however, that occurred somewhere between thirty thousand and forty thousand years ago. Not only did man invent fire, speech, and abstract thought, he also invented weapons. There is some evidence in the fossil record for cannibalism in the life of early man at this stage of his development. Surely such behavior was not bequeathed to us by the gods!

It is interesting that von Däniken does not question what humankind has obviously developed on its own over the last five hundred years or so. He allows archaeologists and historians to explain the events that led from the voyages of Columbus to the landing of men on the moon on the basis of human capacities and the normal interactions between men and their environments. It is only those civilizations that had not yet developed writing that he finds populated with outer-space gods whose exploits became legend and were recorded in writing only later. Should it not be the other way around? Would not the civilizations in contact with the 'gods' be the most advanced and capable of recording their visits? And as we began to reach to the level at which we would communicate better with our space-gods, why did they stop getting in touch with us?

Von Däniken's appreciation of history is as lacking as his knowledge of genetics. He makes no reference to the enormous amount of research showing man's steady progress from stone tools that were simple chopping implements to the development, thousands of years later, of finely chipped spear points. He ignores the thousands of years that were involved in the domestication of plants and animals. In Mexico, the domestication of plants led from a hunting and gathering society, in which wild corn and other edible plants were collected, to village life, which depended on the growing of plants. This transition took over three thousand years to complete, from about 5000 B.C. to about 1500 B.C. It took place, furthermore, not near a likely place for outer-space contact, but in a highland area, where the plants that were domesticated grew wild.

Von Däniken also fails to appreciate the process by which advances accumulate; development after development, idea after idea, advances build upon one another, slowly at first, then gradually accelerating, until in recent times, inventions take place so fast we can hardly keep up with them.*

Of course, certain breakthroughs occur which bring about a rapid series of changes. Take, for example, the industrial revolution that began in England in the 1750s, which revolu-

---

* No one need take the word of only one person on this subject, whether it is von Däniken or any individual archaeologist. The reader may want to check other accounts of man's development.

tionized production and distribution of commodities and eventually the social structure of all societies on earth. It happened rapidly. It was a time of an amazing variety of inventions and new ideas: steam engines, railroads, the cotton gin, mass production. Can they all have been invented by mere men?

If von Däniken is concerned with where the narrators of *The Thousand and One Nights* got their 'staggering wealth of ideas',[5] then the industrial revolution must be a real trouble spot for him. And what of today? Who could possibly have thought of computers, laser beams, or nuclear reactors? Are these not the questions that von Däniken would be likely to ask if he were around a thousand years in the future?

5

The Piri Re'is Map

One of von Däniken's most interesting claims is that certain ancient maps must have been based on aerial photographs taken by astronaut-gods over South America, the Atlantic Ocean, and Africa. Though he retracted this claim in the interview cited earlier for *Playboy* magazine,[1] millions of von Däniken's readers are not aware of this. In fact, von Däniken repeats this assertion in his later book *In Search of Ancient Gods:* 'To me it is obvious that extraterrestrial spacemen made the maps from space stations in orbit.'[2]

In spite of the plural term 'maps', which he uses inconsistently, von Däniken is referring to one map in particular, which is reproduced in the pictorial section of *Chariots of the Gods?* Furthermore, the map, dated 1513, was not discovered in the eighteenth century, as von Däniken says,* but in the year 1929, when the palace of Topkapu (or the old Imperial Palace of Constantinople) was being converted into a museum. It was found by B. Halil Etem Eldem, the Director of National Museums at the time. The map attracted the attention of scholars, and a report was published in 1931.[3]

The 1513 map was interesting from the standpoint of its

---

* Von Däniken correctly states the date of discovery of the Piri Re'is map in his later book *In Search of Ancient Gods.*

rather good accuracy *for the sixteenth century*, but was especially interesting because the mapmaker, Piri Re'is (or Piri Ibn Haji Mehmed, as his name appears on the map), states in a marginal note that he based part of it on a map drawn by Columbus. This sounded like the legendary 'lost map of Columbus', which would probably be the oldest map of America, assuming other ancient navigators had not been there first. Piri Re'is (pronounced 'Peeree Ry-iss') was a former pirate who later became an admiral in the Turkish Navy. His uncle was the famous Kemal Re'is, who also happened to be an admiral, which may have had something to do with Piri's official promotion.

At any rate, the Piri Re'is map eventually found its way to M. I. Walters of the U.S. Navy Hydrographic Office in 1956, and from there to Captain Arlington H. Mallery, a student of old maps. Mallery examined the map and ventured the opinion that the lower portion represented bays and islands of the coast of Antarctica, which is now, of course, under an icecap. Walters, with Mallery's agreement, participated in a radio panel discussion on 26 August 1956, with the Reverend Daniel L. Linehan, S.J., director of the Weston Observatory of Boston College. This broadcast came to the attention of Charles H. Hapgood, who became interested and later initiated a study in conjunction with his history of science class at Keene State College in New Hampshire.[4] The results of this study are detailed in his book *Maps of the Ancient Sea Kings*.

Here is what von Däniken has said about the Piri Re'is map of 1513:

> Mallery and Walters constructed a grid and transferred the maps to a modern globe. They made a sensational discovery. The maps were absolutely accurate – and not only as regards the Mediterranean and the Dead Sea. The coasts of North and South America and even the contours of the Antarctic were also precisely delineated on Piri Reis' [*sic*] maps. . . .
> The latest studies of Professor Charles H. Hapgood and mathematician Richard W. Strachan give us some more shattering information. Comparison with modern photographs of our

globe taken from satellites showed that the originals of Piri Re'is [*sic*] maps must have been aerial photographs taken from a very great height. . . . Unquestionably our forefathers did not draw these maps. Yet there is no doubt that the maps must have been made with the most modern technical aid – from the air. . . . [5]

Von Däniken's discussion of the Piri Re'is map is one case in which he goes beyond mistaking one thing for another or proposing a bold new theory. His statements that 'The maps were absolutely accurate' and that 'the contours of the Antarctic were also precisely delineated on Piri Re'is maps' are not just matters of interpretation; they are strictly false. The map is not by any means correctly drawn, and the identification of Antarctica without its ice cover is highly dubious.

One has only to look at a clearer representation of the map than the one supplied in *Chariots of the Gods?* to see just how inaccurate the Piri Re'is map really is. Comparisons shown in Hapgood's book between the Piri Re'is version and modern maps of Cuba, Crete, and the western Mediterranean show very little resemblance. Concerning Cuba (large island on upper left of map), Hapgood remarks:

In the first place, Cuba was wrongly labeled *Espaniola* (Hispaniola, the island now comprising Haiti and the Dominican Republic) by Piri Re'is. This error was accepted by Philip Karhle who studied the map in the 1930s. . . . Nothing could better illustrate how ignorant Piri Re'is was of his own map. The mislabeling of Cuba also clearly shows that all he did was to get some information verbally from a sailor captured by his uncle, or from some other source, and then try to fit the information to a map already in his possession, a map he may have found in the Turkish Naval Archives, which possibly inherited it from the Byzantine Empire. . . . I have compared the island I have identified on the Piri Re'is map as Cuba with a modern map of that island.

This comparison shows that what we have . . . on the Peri Re'is Map is a map of Cuba, but a map only of its eastern half. [6]

Other specific errors are the omission of about nine hundred miles of South American coastline, a duplication of the

Amazon River, and the omission of the Drake Passage between Cape Horn and the Antarctic Peninsula, the latter representing nine degrees on the map. Moreover, the section of the map identified by Mallery and Hapgood as part of Queen Maud Land does not show a 'striking agreement' with

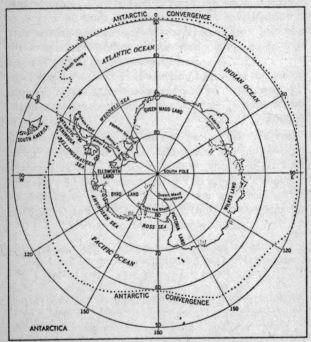

Recent map of the land mass below the Antarctic icecap. Any similarity between the Palmer and Queen Maud Land areas and the southernmost portion of the Piri Re'is map is less than striking. *From Gazetteer No. 14, August 1966, Office of Geography, Department of the Interior, Washington, D.C.*

the seismic profile of this area.[7] All these discrepancies would seem to rule out the map's having been derived from an aerial photograph.

In spite of von Däniken's implication, Hapgood did not suggest that the Piri Re'is map, or any other ancient maps he studied, were made from the air. For example, in reference to the Andes mountain range on the western side of South America, Hapgood states: ' . . . the drawing of the mountains indicates that they were observed from the sea – from coastwise shipping.'[8] What Hapgood did theorize was that 'some ancient people explored the coasts of Antarctica when its coasts were free of ice'.[9]

The Piri Re'is map, although not 'proof' of extraterrestrial visitations, remains a fascinating subject for study, especially when considered along with other old maps that show a continent suggestive of Antarctica. To Hapgood, these maps, and the ancient maps on which they were based, indicate a lost civilization with advanced knowledge of navigation and mapmaking, but he does not attribute such a civilization to outer-space 'gods'. Von Däniken has done Hapgood somewhat of a disservice by implicating him in the ancient astronaut controversy.

As I have indicated earlier in this book, von Däniken's ideas, which he likes to call his 'theory', are not original (as he finally admitted in the *Playboy* interview published in August 1974). As early as 1960 (i.e. eight years prior to the publication of von Däniken's first book), at least three authors were promoting the same theory based on the same faulty claims. These were Louis Pauwels and Jacques Bergier in *The Morning of the Magicians* and Donald Keyhoe in *Flying Saucers: Top Secret*. Even von Däniken's device of employing a barrage of rhetorical questions to make a point seems to have come from Pauwels and Bergier. These sentences from *The Morning of the Magicians* illustrate the parallel: 'Were these copies of earlier maps? Had they been traced from observations made on board a flying machine or space vessel of some kind? Notes taken by visitors from Beyond? We shall doubtless be criticized for asking these questions.'[10]

Keyhoe gives his account in dialogue style through the personage of one 'Captain Brent' (since Keyhoe tells us in his book that he has changed the names of certain individuals, we do not know who this man really is).

'Have you ever thought,' Captain Brent asked me quietly, 'that the earth might be a colony started by another world?'

I looked at him, startled. 'I've heard it suggested but – do you actually believe it?'

'I'm certain of this much,' replied Brent. 'A race far more technically advanced than we are today was on earth thousands of years ago.'

He swung around to a cabinet, took out a folder. 'The Hydrographic Office of the Navy has verified an ancient chart – it's called the Piri Re'is map – that goes back more than 5,000 years. It's so accurate only one thing could explain it – a worldwide *aerial* [*sic*] survey.'[11]

Then in 1963, the story of the Piri Re'is map's being the product of an advanced civilization in contact with the earth appeared in Robert Charroux's *One Hundred Thousand Years of Man's Unknown History*. What all these books have in common is their unreliability, as exemplified by such basic errors as the time of the map's discovery. Von Däniken tells us it was discovered at the beginning of the eighteenth century. Pauwels and Bergier said it was in the middle of the nineteenth century and that Piri Re'is himself presented it to the Library of Congress.[12] According to Charroux, it was found in the Topkapu Palace in Istanbul as recently as 1957.[13]

6

The Nazca Plain

Between the towns of Nazca and Palpa, in southern Peru, lies a region of desert more than forty miles long and averaging nine miles wide that was, quite literally, a gigantic drawing board for its ancient inhabitants. There, discernable only from the air, are found enormous straight lines, trapezoids, triangles, spirals, and the outlines of animals: birds, fish, lizards, a spider, and a monkey. The markings, made between 400 B.C. and A.D. 900, were etched into the desert floor by removing the surface stones to expose the lighter subsoil.

To von Däniken, the geometric designs looked like landing strips, probably for interplanetary aircraft. Again, as in most other cases of his alleged evidence for the space-god theory, the original idea was not his own.

Although the concept did appear in *The Morning of the Magicians* (in 1960), it had been offered previously in George Hunt Williamson's *Road in the Sky* as a complete chapter entitled 'Beacons for the Gods'.[1] And again, von Däniken gives little credit to these earlier authors.

Here is von Däniken's presentation:

> If you fly over this territory – the plain of Nazca – you can make out gigantic lines, laid out geometrically, some of which run parallel to each other, while others intersect or are sur-

rounded by large trapezoidal areas.

The archaeologists say that they are Inca roads.

A preposterous idea! Of what use to the Incas were roads that ran parallel to each other? That intersected? That were laid out in a plain and came to a sudden end?...

Seen from the air, the clear-cut impression that the 37-mile-long plain of Nazca made on *me* [italics his] was that of an airfield![2]

Even though previous authors of the ancient-airfield theory are easily found in the popular literature of ten and fifteen years ago, it is not so easy to find references to archaeologists who ever seriously considered the Nazca lines as Inca roads. In fact, the first archaeologist to investigate the lines, the late Paul Kosok of Long Island University, ruled out this possibility in his first article on the subject, published in 1947. In this preliminary report, entitled 'The Mysterious Markings of Nazca', Kosok pointed out that although the present inhabitants of the Nazca area sometimes referred to the markings as Inca Roads, 'their very nature, size, and position indicate that they could never have been used for ordinary purposes of transportation'.[3]

Dr Kosok was the first to investigate the strange desert markings. In 1939, while studying ancient irrigation systems on the coast of Peru, he noticed that one of the lines coincided with the point on the horizon where the sun set on the day of the winter solstice in the Southern Hemisphere (i.e. the shortest day of the year). This discovery led Kosok to theorize that the lines represented a gigantic astronomical calendar.

A brief study of the lines were reported in 1973 by astronomer Gerald Hawkins of Boston University in his book *Beyond Stonehenge*. After making computer calculations of significant alignments of a selected number of lines at different dates in the ancient past, Hawkins concluded that the solar, lunar, and stellar alignments were no better than what would be expected by chance. But mathematician Maria Reiche, who has studied the Nazca lines for nearly thirty years, still believes in the calendar theory, and at least one American astronomer, William Hartmann of the Planetary Science Institute in Tuscon, Arizona, partially agrees with her.

In a recent conversation I had with Hartmann, he suggested that the lines may not represent a single undertaking at one particular point in time. When Hawkins fed into the computer the question: 'What stars did the lines point to at any date between 5000 B.C. and A.D. 1900?' he says, 'The print-out sheets were full, stars at the end of each line.'⁴ But Hawkins rejects the significance of this finding, because he requires that the lines 'hang together' in any given century; that is, for each century investigated, the number of alignments should be more than would be expected by chance for the number of lines, or directions, tested. Furthermore, Hawkins' study was not geared to detect other *kinds* of alignments, such as how the shadows of certain hills and ridges, marked by the lines, might also prove to be significant.

It is interesting that certain of the animal figures laid out on the Nazca plain almost perfectly coincide (leaving some room for human error) with some of the ancient constellations over the Southern Hemisphere. The constellation of Pavo, the Peacock, can be seen superimposed on the outline of a bird, identified as a condor, 'drawn' on the plain. The stars fit the condor in much the same manner as the northern star patterns line up with their mythical counterparts. Perhaps the Nazca figures were representations of constellations recognized at the time. This hypothesis supports Maria Reiche's suggestion that the large figures were drawn from reduced models; the models might have been the star patterns that form the outlines of the subjects represented. The fact that the Nazca configurations are seen only from the air is consistent with the ancient desire that the gods in the sky notice the peoples below. And what would make the people more noticeable to them (at a time without electric lights or radio signals) than giant pictorial representations of certain forms of life indigenous to their own particular region of the earth? Even von Däniken admits that the ancients *already* worshipped the sun and the moon *before* 'the gods [came] down from heaven'.[5]

Whether these mysterious markings represent constellations, ceremonial pathways, an astronomical calendar, or something quite different, we do not know. But one thing is fairly certain, and that is the absurdity of the ancient-airfield theory.

Some of the reasons counting against it are the following: (1) It hardly seems reasonable that advanced extraterrestrial spacecraft would require *landing strips*. Certainly NASA's Lunar Excursion Modules come straight down on the surface. I always thought that 'flying saucers' were supposed to do that, too. What were the ancient astronauts flying – World War I biplanes? (It also seems odd that while postulating landing strips for horizontally operational spacecraft, von Däniken also supports the vertical-lander theory of Josef Blumrich.) (2) Some of these strips are five miles long, and others run right into hills and ridges. It would be a bouncy ride, to say the least. (3) A spaceport requiring a pilot to get his bearings from configurations that can be seen only during the day would make landings very difficult at night. And since no broken pieces of ancient lightbulbs have been found I assume there were no landing lights. (4) The soft, sandy soil of the Nazca pampa is hardly the kind of surface that would be required for an airport. As Maria Reiche has said, 'I'm afraid the spacemen would have gotten stuck.'[6]

But the question is still asked: why would the early Peruvians go to the trouble of constructing designs of such size and precision – designs they could not appreciate without an aerial vantage point?

The Miami-based International Explorers Society has suggested that the Nazcans might have been able to see the markings from aloft in hot-air balloons. Michael Debakey, director of the I.E.S., theorized that ancient man could have grasped the concept of an airship simply by noticing how smoke from a campfire rises into the air.[7] If the smoke could be captured, it might carry a man along with it.

On a piece of Nazcan pottery is a picture that resembles a hot-air bag. And, archives at the University of Coimbra in Portugal indicate that smoke balloons may have been used by the Indians of South America prior to the advent of ballooning in Europe. In ancient grave sites at Nazca, finely woven textiles were discovered that could have made good envelopes for such balloons. If the balloon was filled with smoke, the inside surfaces of the fabric would become coated with soot and would thus be able to hold in the required amount of heated air for flight. Interestingly enough, evidence of several huge burn pits can be seen on the Nazca 'runways'. Debakey thinks that such a balloon might have been flown on ceremonial occasions by Nazcan priests. Furthermore, this theory would help explain the construction of the ground markings; riders in the ballon may have guided the Nazcan artists as they laid out the designs, as suggested in *The Morning of the Magicians*.[8]

In November 1975, two members of the I.E.S. actually flew a crude hot-air balloon over the plain of Nazca to prove their point.[9] It was a remarkable example of experimental archaeology, in which a hypothetical structure is created using materials similar to those available to ancient man. The 80,000-cubic-foot, seven-story balloon named, appropriately, *Condor I*, carried two passengers, Julian Nott, a British balloonist, and Jim Woodman of Miami, to an altitude of 600 feet. Nott and Woodman rode in a gondola-basket made of totora reeds from the shores of Lake Titicaca, held by lines and fastenings also made of native fibers. The envelope of the balloon was constructed of a finely woven fabric similar to the textiles uncovered at Nazca. The smoke and hot air were supplied from coals in a clay pot.

Although this experiment certainly does not constitute proof that the Nazcans could fly, it does suggest an intriguing alternative to the space-god theory to account for the strange lines.

7

Easter Island

One of von Däniken's most blatant distortions of archaeological findings is in the case of Easter Island. To anyone
who has read Thor Heyerdahl's *Aku-Aku* it is quite evident
that von Däniken has not told the whole truth about the
carving and erection of the giant statues. Here, again, he
has conveniently ignored information that would spoil his
argument. After reading Heyerdahl's account of the actual
raising of a statue by descendents of the Easter Island
sculptors, he was, he admits, 'prepared to cross an unsolved
puzzle off [his] list as solved'.[1] But then, standing in front of
the lava wall in the crater from which the statues were
carved, he 'decided to let the question mark stay on [his]
list'.[2] His reason: 'Nobody could ever have freed such
gigantic lumps of lava with small, primitive stone tools. Thor
Heyerdahl made the natives hammer away for weeks with
the old implements which were found in abundance. I saw
the meager result: a groove of a few inches in the hard
volcanic rock!'[3]

Actually, the mayor of Easter Island and six of his men
carved out the contours of a new statue in three days with
the old stone tools. As Heyerdahl relates, they 'hacked and
cut parallel depressions down the face of the rock, then they
cut across the edge left between the furrows, breaking it

off into pieces. They cut and cut and flung on water [to soften the rock] and continually they changed their picks, for the points soon blunted'.⁴ However, the work was hard, and it was estimated that it would take about a year for two teams of six men working all day in shifts to complete a medium-size statue. But it could be done.

In rejecting Heyerdahl's belief that stone tools were used to carve the statues, von Däniken was left with the problem of explaining the presence of hundreds of stone picks around the quarry. This called for another of his admittedly 'fantastic' scenarios. It seems that some 'intelligent beings' became stranded on Easter Island. While awaiting rescue, they relieved their boredom by constructing the famous statues, using advanced stoneworking techniques. Then their people came for them, and they abandoned their work. After their departure, the Easter Islanders tried to complete the unfinished statues using their own primitive tools, but finding the task impossible, flung them down. 'I claim,' says von Däniken, 'that the stone tools are evidence of resignation in the face of a task that could not be mastered.'⁵ If his scenario is fantastic, his argument is audacious. Not only has he tried to explain away formidable evidence; he has attempted to use it to 'prove exactly the opposite' of what it would appear to indicate.

However, von Däniken does not seem to question the Easter Islanders' ability to place atop the statues the red stone 'hats' they 'wore' before they were knocked down. In the 'hats' he finds another mystery that can be explained by a visit from the 'gods':

> . . . why were the red hats put on the strange statues at all? So, far, I have not found a convincing explanation in the whole of the literature about Easter Island. So I ask myself the following questions:
>   Had the islanders seen 'gods' with helmets and remembered the fact when it came to making statues?
>   Was that the reason why the statues did not seem complete to them without the hat-helmets?⁶

Here is Heyerdahl's explanation given nearly twenty years

ago: 'Actually, it is not quite correct to talk about hats, even though everyone does so nowadays. The old native name for this gigantic head decoration is *pukao*, which means "topknot", the usual coiffure worn by male natives on Easter Island at the time of its discovery."

Since von Däniken has so badly misrepresented the archaeology of Easter Island and so boldly challenged the work of Thor Heyerdahl, I invited Dr Heyerdahl to answer von Däniken by way of a written statement to be quoted verbatim in this book. And so I include here Thor Heyerdahl's own comments in response to that request:

Throughout the world a large number of seriously working scientists do a painstaking job in unraveling fragments of information which may help mankind reconstruct the forgotten history of his own eventful past. Unfortunately, many of these scholars have been brought up with the old-fashioned view that their findings only concern their fellow scientists, and publishing their discoveries and results in technical volumes, they make little or no effort to reach the common man in the street. This hard-dying attitude is slowly changing as we approach the end of the twentieth century, but in the meantime the market has been wide open for a number of unscrupulous writers who, with or without guilty conscience, have accumulated wealth and fame by feeding the innocent public with what they feel the public would like to hear. Most fruitful of these writers are those who are up to date with modern moon travels and reverse the issue by hoaxed stories of people from space who have already called upon our planet. The achievement of modern man having reached our own satellite, the moon, is so fantastic that the man in the street finds nothing incredible anymore.

Serious scientists smile at the unrestricted credibility of the untrained layman. Whereas they may quarrel among themselves about details of a technical nature and theories of reconstruction, no scientist takes people like von Däniken seriously, and none of them cares to climb down from the academic pedestal to start discussing sheer nonsense merely to enlighten the man in the street. With or without reason, the feeling among those who could combat the world-sweeping hoaxes has been: Anyone stupid enough to take this kind of hoax seriously deserves to be cheated. And while millions of people are made fools by the silence of the scholars and the unhampered publicity campaigns of the hoax-makers, scientists go on writing for themselves, and at best comment on von Däniken and his like with a passing joke. For instance, one scholar came back from Egypt with the following comment: 'I start to believe that the ancient Egyptians actually had wireless, we have been digging for years everywhere and never found a single wire!'

Personally I organized and led the first archaeological expedition ever to carry out stratigraphic excavations on Easter Island. A professional team of American and European archaeologists worked with me for six months on the island, and up to a hundred workmen at a time were engaged in our excavations. Together we published two huge scientific volumes on the results, apart from a popular report on our adventures, *Aku-Aku*, which I wrote for interested laymen. Von Däniken subsequently wrote such books as *Chariots of the Gods?* and *Return to the Stars* [*Gods from Outer Space*], etc., where he totally ignored these findings and publications and concocted sheer nonsense to satisfy and entertain his space-hungry readers. Together with my colleagues, I am to blame for not promptly having used the modern mass media for telling the public not to take his reference to Easter Island seriously. However, like other scholars, we did not foresee that people would take his concoctions more seriously than we did ourselves, and it is never pleasant to launch public attacks if not in direct self-defense. Therefore our silence.

The general reader who cares to know has the right to be informed that there is not the slightest base of fact in what von Däniken writes concerning the origin of the giant statues on Easter Island. We know exactly how they were carved, where they were carved, why they were carved, and when they were carved. The last statues were carved about A.D.1680, when a civil war on the island interrupted all work in the image quarries of the extinct volcano Rano Raraku, near the eastern corner of the island. Thousands of crude stone adzes and picks used for the work were still found scattered about in the quarries, and the local islanders recalled how their own ancestors had carved, transported, and erected the statues, which were raised as monuments for deceased kings and chiefs. They actually showed us how to carve a giant with the abandoned basalt tools, and how to move it on skids and erect it through an ingenious underbuilding of stones. This year, after twenty years of continuous research on the remarkable pre-history of Easter Island and the origin of its people, I am publishing the final volume on the results in a richly illustrated book, *The Art of Easter Island*. This tome will hardly reach many general readers, nor would they need to know very much about

Easter Island archaeology to judge the value of von Däniken's conclusions for themselves.

If civilized beings had come from outer space to Easter Island, or to ancient Peru or Egypt for that matter, they, like our moon travelers, would need spaceships and accessories of such incredible durability that they could resist the immense heat of friction when descending through our atmosphere. Why, then, the intelligent layman should ask himself, is no fragment of such metal, plastic, or other fabric of the sort ever found where the ancient spacemen supposedly landed and worked, but only stone and bone tools good enough to do the job but not brought from other planets?

We the scientists are to be blamed for not speaking up, the uninformed laymen are to be blamed for not using their own common sense, and commercial writers like von Däniken are to be blamed for not telling their readers that they are selling them entertaining fiction and not popular-science books.

August 4, 1975   THOR HEYERDAHL.

Heyerdahl, in *Aku-Aku*, makes many references to three members of the famous expedition of 1955–56: Dr William Mulloy of the University of Wyoming. Dr Carlyle Smith of the University of Kansas, and Edwin Ferdon, formerly of the Museum of New Mexico but now associate director of the Arizona State Museum at the University of Arizona. It was my good fortune to meet Edwin Ferdon on 19 May 1975, at the Arizona State Museum, where, after a brief discussion of the books of Erich von Däniken, the following interview took place:

STORY: Mr Ferdon, one of the aspects of Easter Island that von Däniken purports to be an unearthly mystery is how the *moai*, the giant statues, could possibly have been carved out of 'steel-hard' volcanic rock.[8] Can you shed some light on this enigma?

FERDON: The big statues, the typical ones, are carved out of a volcanic tuff which is a volcanic ash with inclusions in it. Now, to carve this is not very difficult. We ran an experiment there. We had the mayor and some of his men go over to outline a small statue. We wanted to see how they handled carving. They are working with

63

hand picks, and the fascinating thing is that these hand picks, which were of a tear-drop design, would be used until they got dull. The men would line them up until they had several. The mayor would then go over there, grab another rock and flake a new point on each pick. And so he just kept the supply going for his men. The trick of carving this stuff was this: First, they all had a gourd of water. They had found that if you moistened the surface of this volcanic ash, it became a little softer. So they got their working area wetted down. Second, we usually think of hacking out something by pecking all over the surface of it. But there is a more efficient way of doing it, and they do it. They peck down in a line until it is, say, an inch deep. They move over, and peck another line, maybe one-half or three-quarters of an inch over. Now you have two grooves with a keel in the middle. Then you go down and knock out the keel. It goes down much faster that way. The whole operation, you see, is not as hard as you might think.

STORY: About transporting the statues; in *Aku-Aku* it is said that about 180 natives were needed to pull a twelve-ton statue, using ropes tied around its neck.

FERDON: To begin with, they had to pull it out of deep sand, but once it got up onto the hard soil, we could have cut that crew down by at least one-half. Once they got out of the sand, they really started tearing with this thing, and we had to stop them, or they would have pulled it away from the actual site.

STORY: Heyerdahl mentions a wooden sledge that was used.

FERDON: Yes, they had the wooden sledge under it, and it held up beautifully. They must have pulled it a hundred yards before we stopped them.

STORY: Von Däniken says in his *Chariots of the Gods?* that 'No trees grow on the island, which is a tiny speck of volcanic stone. The usual explanation, that the stone giants were moved to their present sites on wooden rollers, is not feasible in this case.'* In *Gods from*

---

* No archaeologist, as far as I know, has claimed the statues were moved on rollers.

Outer Space, he writes that archaeologists have said 'that no finds [have] yet supplied proof that the islanders had ever had wood at their disposal as building material (for rollers)'.[10] But I notice that William Mulloy has shed some new light on the matter in his article 'A Speculative Reconstruction of Techniques of Carving, Transporting and Erecting Easter Island Statues'. He says that 'Vegetation in historic times has been principally short grass with a few scrub trees. As yet unpublished pollen studies have revealed that a much heavier cover formerly existed, including large trees and many plant species now locally extinct. This more dense vegetation eventually may have been cleared to exhaustion for agricultural plantations as population increased."[11]

FERDON: Yes. In fact, there were even trees reported by Captain Cook in the latter half of the eighteenth century. And trees imported on the island grow beautifully today.

STORY: The sled that was used to transport the statue, then, was within the reach of the early islanders?

FERDON: Yes. The fork of a tree is what it was – designed to form a sledge. The runners were expanded out like a 'V.' And that sled was no bigger than what you could have gotten from a tree that did grow fifteen feet tall. So the wood was available. If you didn't cut it out of the fork of a tree, you could have easily taken the trunks of two smaller trees and formed your sled in that manner. So from the point of view of having wood available, there was no problem.

STORY: Continuing from von Däniken's account in *Chariots of the Gods?*, he says, ' . . . the island can scarcely have provided food for more than 2,000 inhabitants. (A few hundred [he says] . . . live on Easter Island today.)"[12]

FERDON: Oh, no – a few hundred!? There are actually about sixteen hundred right now and in prehistoric times there were probably far in excess of three or four thousand. And furthermore, they are growing all the crops they need. You see, the island looks as barren as it can be. But when we were there, I got the rainfall record, and that island, although it looks as though it might be getting fifteen inches a year, is getting about forty-five to fifty inches of rainfall a year. And that is good rainfall, especially for growing taro and sweet potatoes. And they grow sweet potatoes like crazy there. Furthermore, the Air Force gave me the data on frontal storms, and there was at least one frontal storm moving through per month. So you aren't just dependent on the trade winds out there or the rain on one side of the island only. You were getting heavy rainfall all over the island.

STORY: Getting back to the raising of the statues; as I understand it, the statue that was raised near your camp at Anakena was a different one than the one that was transported, and this one weighed even more – about twenty-five or thirty tons. Heyerdahl tells in *Aku-Aku* that it took twelve men eighteen days to do the job. How was this accomplished?

FERDON: First, the men went down to the beach and gathered up all the boulders they could find and brought them in near the statue. Then they brought in three long poles, which, again, could have been easily obtained by the prehistoric islanders with the type of forest they had. Then they started working on one long side of the statue. They don't work on either end; they put the fulcrum very low on the log and stay on the long sides of the statue only. So they were getting a terrific advantage. The leverage is fantastic. These men would start pulling down on the pole, and you would then hear a kind of creaking noise. The statue would have gone up a little, and they would immediately throw in some boulders. Then they would go around on the other long side of the statue and repeat the performance. They just kept going back and forth on each side until the thing was up in the air. Now, this was quite a distance from the actual platform [or *ahu*]. And so part of this process, once you got the statue above the ground, was to lever and move. And you are not only raising the statue, but you are moving it forward, you see, as you go along. Then, when the thing got high enough, they had to fasten ropes to the ends of their poles so they could pull on the ropes, but again, there was this one man always up by the statue, and whenever there was a little creaking, he simply rearranged the boulders and pushed them farther back under the statue to take advantage of that.

We are so used to a derrick dropping down with a cable, and seeing half a building move –

STORY: Because we are always in a hurry to get the job done.

FERDON: Yes, and they weren't. The whole thing is leverage and it just went beautifully. They pointed out exactly where they were going to put the statue, and that's exactly where it ended up. There was a rock platform all ready for it. It was moved directly in place, horizontally with the boulder platform, and then they began working near the head, back and forth.

STORY: In other words, they had it raised on the boulders up to the level of the platform with the statue still in the horizontal position *before* raising it vertically?

FERDON: They got it up even with the platform, and then they started working back on the other end.

STORY: Then they could really have raised one on a platform thirty feet high by just piling enough rocks under it?

FERDON: Oh, yes, and none of these platforms were that high. I notice that Däniken talks about the 'hats'. Well, you stop and think a minute. You already have a large platform made. So you simply start wedging up your hat, up that rocky mass, making it higher as you need to. And the hats aren't that heavy. The hats are made of a red volcanic ash, and if anything, they are lighter than the volcanic ash of the statue.

STORY: Von Däniken entitles his chapter in *Chariots of the*

Gods? 'Easter Island – Land of the Bird Men' and says: 'An orally transmitted legend tells us that flying men landed and lighted fires in ancient times. The legend is confirmed by sculptures of flying creatures with big, staring eyes.'[13] In *Aku-Aku* there is an illustration (on page 161) of a bird-man figure, and I see that you have a photo of them carved on a cliff overlooking some islands. Heyerdahl says in his book that you were working at that location, the cult center Orongo. What are the bird-men all about?

FERDON: Yes, this is why I chose this particular site, which happens to be nine hundred feet above the sea. Once a year, all the tribal chiefs would assemble there for a ceremony. This began apparently at the time when the sooty tern moved into Easter Island and began to nest on those islands over there. After a certain amount of ceremony, the high chief of the total island would give a signal, and swimmers representing each chief, or the chiefs themselves, would then try to get off the island as fast as possible. A few would dive off the nine-hundred-foot cliff; some of them never made it. The idea was to get the first egg of the year laid by the sooty tern. The man that got it received all the *mana*, or supernatural power, that any human being could have. This means that nobody could touch him or his tribe. Now, he had a rough life. He ended up having to live in a house and be fed for the entire year. He couldn't move around because he had too much *mana*. And this lasted for one year. Then, the next year, the ceremony was repeated.

In his attempt to discredit Heyerdahl's findings, von Däniken states that 'archaeologists all over the world protested against this example'[14] (the demonstration of the moving of the statues). This is just not true. It has been generally accepted that the methods demonstrated by the mayor, Atan, and his men for the Heyerdahl expedition are similar to those used in ancient times.

Professor Mulloy, who, with Ferdon, witnessed the Heyerdahl demonstration in 1955, suggests that a fork sledge with a 'curved undersurface similar to that of a rocking chair'[15] would be even more efficient than the one made by the mayor. Mulloy's experiments with a scale model of Paro, the largest statue (about eighty-two tons) ever carved and transported by the early Easter Islanders, showed that 'the weight of the relatively light though long head would be countered by the concentrated weight in the projecting belly so that the statue would balance almost horizontally on the sledge with the head elevated above the ground and the delicate surfaces of the latter would be undamaged in movement'.[16] The cordage used could well have been the local *hau* (*Triumfetta semitriloba*) bast, which would produce a very strong and suitable fiber. 'With knowledge of cord twisting, cables of any size necessary could have been pro-

A speculative reconstruction of techniques for carving, transporting, and erecting Easter Island statues by William Mulloy. *Reprinted by permission from Archaeology & Physical Anthropology in Oceania, vol. 5, no. 1 (April 1970). Drawings by William Mulloy*

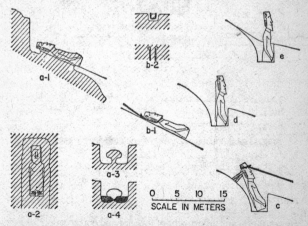

Details of carving and lowering statue to foot of talus. *a-1*, statue attached to living rock by longitudinal level; *a-2*, channel carved around statue; *a-3, 4*, technique of severing keel; *b-1*, lowering statue with restraint by cable; *b-2*, snubbing device; *c, d, e*, erection of statue in pit at foot at talus

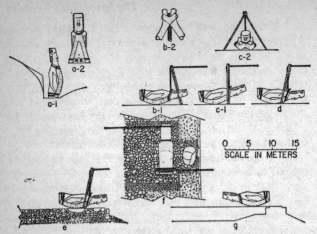

Transportation of statue. *a-1, 2*, attachment of fork sledge; *b–d*, transportation with bipod; *e*, position of statue at arrival at *ahu*; *f*, reversal of position; *g*, statue ready for adjustment of topknot and erection

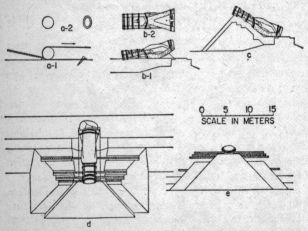

Transportation and adjustment of topknot and construction for first phase of erection of statue. *a-1*, transportation of statue with lever and parbuckle; *a-2*, section of topknot as transported and after recarving and cutting mortise; *b-1, 2*, attachment of topknot and tilting of statue to receive it; *c*, lateral view of masonry for first phase of erection; *d, e*, front and overhead views of same

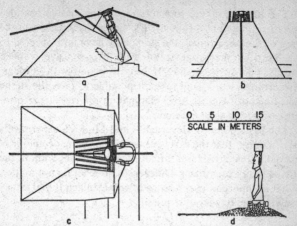

Second phase of erection of statue. *a–c*, lateral, front, and overhead views of erection masonry; *d*, erected statue with masonry platform removed

duced easily by several men co-operating in the re-twisting of light ropes by hand."[17]

After the statue has been lashed to the fork sledge, another measure can be taken that is more mechanically advantageous than simply pulling it along: use of a bipod. The bipod arrangement suggested itself to Mulloy when he thought about the traditional explanation given by the natives that the statues 'walked' and 'stopped', traveling a small distance each day, until they reached their destination. The bipod would act as a primitive type of crane, supporting the weight of the statue and allowing a movement suggestive of 'walking' and 'stopping' just as the ancient legend says.

Professor Mulloy thinks that the levering of the statues into position was probably done against a wooden armature of some sort to prevent them from being damaged. In 1960 Mulloy and another archaeologist, Gonzalo Figueroa of the University of Chile, restored and re-erected seven statues, weighing approximately sixteen tons each, in a manner similar to Atan's, again without the use of heavy equipment.

The placing of the topknots on statues' heads has also been considered by Mulloy. He believes that, at least in the case of the larger *moai*, the stone may have been secured to the head of the prone statue with two concave wooden beams, one on each side. If heavily bound with cordage, this arrangement would make it possible to raise the statue and topknot together, thus eliminating the repeat performance of raising a second stone.

The basic point of Heyerdahl's and Mulloy's experiments is, of course, that the early Easter Island natives *could have* carved, transported, and raised the giant statues without the use of heavy equipment. Differences in detail do not matter. What is important in reference to von Däniken is that outer-space technology is not required.

8

The Egyptian Pyramids

In support of his ancient astronaut hypothesis, von Däniken makes an astonishing claim: that 'ancient Egypt appears suddenly and without transition with a fantastic ready-made civilization', and that it is 'without recognizable prehistory!'¹ Is he serious? If he had looked at almost any *one* of the approximately twenty thousand volumes of books and periodicals that have been written on the subject, he would have realized the absurdity of such a statement. Specialists in Egyptology from all over the world have excavated in Egypt for more than a hundred years, and have constructed a sequence of prehistory that starts with primitive farmers at Fayum at around 5000 B.C. and continues unbroken until written history.

It is simply not true that the 'pyramids . . . and many other wonderful things shot out of the ground, so to speak'.² Like other aspects of civilization, pyramid-building was the product of many developments, one idea leading to another. To appreciate just how gradually pyramid construction techniques evolved, we must look back to prehistoric times. Before there were tombs, there were burial mounds. These were piles of loose stones, heaped up perhaps to mark the sites, but probably for more practical reasons. In Egypt the desert wind would blow away the soft sand of a grave,

73

leaving the partially exposed body to foraging jackals.

To improve the grave coverings, the first mastabas, made of mud brick, came into being. These early structures were at first nothing more than raised rectangular slabs. As time went on, improvements were made and embellishments added. Chambers were built on the inside in increasing numbers. Later when techniques of working limestone improved, the mastabas were constructed of stone instead of brick.

The first development toward the pyramid-shaped design was the erection of the mastaba in several graduated steps. After this had been done, it was a fairly simple matter, at least on a relatively small scale, to fill in between the steps to form a true pyramid. It apparently was realized at some point that what could be done with a small model could be done on a much larger scale.

The Step Pyramid of Zoser is actually six mastabas stacked one on the other. After that came the first true pyramid — the ruined Pyramid of Meidum. Interestingly enough, it is the partially ruined state of the Meidum pyramid that provides a case for Kurt Mendelssohn's theory that true pyramid-building may have lasted only one century instead of four hundred years, as was previously believed.[3]

Mendelssohn, a retired Oxford University physicist who recently undertook an extensive study of the Egyptian pyramids, believes that the Meidum pyramid collapsed in the third phase of its construction. This early pyramid had stepped interior structure of irregularly shaped stones. The weight of these stones would, of course, exert a downward pressure on the lower layers, but they would also exert an outward pressure. Consequently, the outer layers collapsed and rolled down into a gigantic pile of rubble. This disaster prompted the Egyptian architects to make an abrupt change in the slope of the Pyramid of Dahshur (now known as the 'Bent Pyramid'), reducing it from fifty-four degrees to forty-two degrees. Later pyramids were built entirely of massive, carefully cut blocks.

The important implication for Mendelssohn is that this

sudden change in plan proves that at least two of the largest pyramids were under construction at the same time and suggests that the five largest pyramids may have been built in a single century.⁴ But for our argument here, the example of the partially collapsed Meidum pyramid and subsequent correction of the Bent Pyramid clearly shows a trial-and-error learning process certainly not befitting von Däniken's ancient astronauts.

One curious point about the Egyptian pyramids has been seized upon by von Däniken, his predecessors, and his disciples. It is the supposition that the ratio π (3.14159) was intentionally embodied in the proportions of the Great Pyramid of Cheops, thus indicating that beings of super intelligence designed it.

Eighteenth-century investigators of the Great Pyramid, including Piazzi Smyth, former astronomer royal for Scotland, made extensive measurements of its dimensions. This data seemed to suggest that the height of the pyramid was in relation to the perimeter of its base as the radius of a circle is to its circumference; that is, the perimeter divided by twice the height equals 3.14159, or pi.

In giving this formula in *Chariots of the Gods?* von Däniken substitutes the word 'area' for 'perimeter'.⁵ But no matter; there are other problems. Since the outer casing stones and the tip of the Great Pyramid are missing, it is almost impossible to determine the exact slope of the sides or the true height of the original pyramid. Today we can say only that the slope of the Great Pyramid is approximately fifty-two degrees. And if the margin for error in computing *pi* from the above formula is more than *one minute of arc*, the result of the calculation will *not* be pi.⁵

Another von Däniken idea about the pyramids is that too many people would be required to build them to be fed by Egypt's meager supplies of grain.⁷ But it is a well-known fact that Egypt was the 'breadbasket' for much of the Mediterranean world during classical times, and during most of Rome's history Egypt's grain fed many of the troops in the eastern half of the empire. Julius Caesar and Mark Antony, some have claimed, were more interested in grain for their men than in the charms of Cleopatra.

According to von Däniken, there was no wood in Egypt for rollers (or sledges, which were more likely used) to move the huge stones that went into the great pyramids. However, trade expeditions that returned regularly with cedar wood from Lebanon and other regions are recorded in hiero-glyphic writing.[8] Most of the remains found in Tutan-khamen's tomb were either wood or gold, and wood was used in making many of the everyday items used by Egyptian peasants, such as hoes, which are pictured on tomb walls and temples.

Von Däniken further asks how the blocks for the pyramid were cut from solid rock. The answer is not with lasers, but with harder rock. The quarries where the limestone rock for the large pyramids was extracted have been identified. Here can be seen the rough cut-marks left by stone tools and the evidence of the use of fire cracking and water-based methods of simplifying the cutting of limestone, which is a relatively soft rock.*

Another matter of concern to von Däniken is how the ground on which the Pyramid of Cheops stands was so care-fully and accurately leveled.[9] When I presented this problem to archaeologist William Rathje, of the University of Arizona, he did suggest a possible method. The architects of the pyramids could have built a small dam around the area selected for the base, then filled the area with water, which would naturally seek a level. Next, several holes would be cut down into the bedrock at a set depth from the top of the water. Thus the bottom of each hole would be at the same point below the water throughout the whole area of the pyramid base. The water would be drained and the pyramid base leveled, using the depth of the holes as a guide, by cutting away the rock in between. This is not the superfeat

---

* Many details of possible (and probable) techniques of heavy industry in ancient times can be found in *Archaeology by Experiment*, written by the British archaeologist John Coles (New York: Charles Scribner's Sons, 1973), and in L. Sprague de Camp's *The Ancient Engineers* (Garden City, N.Y.; Doubleday, 1960, 1962, 1963; paperback edition, New York: Ballantine Books, 1974).

of spacemen; it is just something that von Däniken often tends to discount – human ingenuity.

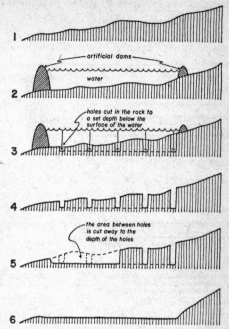

1

2   artificial dams

     water

3   holes cut in the rock to
     a set depth below the
     surface of the water

4

5   the area between holes
     is cut away to the
     depth of the holes

6

A possible method for leveling the base of the Great Pyramid.
Department of Anthropology, University of Arizona

9

The Palenque Astronaut

The personage in this Mayan stone carving from Palenque, Mexico, has achieved an unexpected fame at the hands of von Däniken. His description of the 'rocket-driving god Kukulkan'[1] is convincing in itself.

> There sits a human being, with the upper part of his body bent forward like a racing motorcylist; today any child would identify his vehicle as a rocket. It is pointed at the front, then changes to strangely grooved indentations like inlet ports, widens out, and terminates at the tail in a darting flame. The crouching being himself is manipulating a number of undefinable controls and has the heel of his left foot on a kind of pedal. His clothing is appropriate: short trousers with a broad belt, a jacket with a modern Japanese opening at the neck, and closely fitting bands at arms and legs. With our knowledge of similar pictures, we should be surprised if the complicated headgear were missing. And there it is with the usual indentations and tubes, and something like antennae on top. Our space traveler – he is clearly depicted as one – is not only bent forward tensely; he is also looking intently at an apparatus hanging in front of his face. The astronaut's front seat is separated by struts from the rear portion of the vehicle, in which symmetrically arranged boxes circles, points, and spirals can be seen.[2]

Von Däniken argues that if this example from his 'chain of proofs' is not accepted by scholars, we must doubt their integrity. This is his challenge to honest scholarship. 'A genuinely unprejudiced look at this picture,' he tells us, 'would make even the most die-hard skeptic stop and think.'³ That much may be true, but the illustration of the Palenque carving in von Däniken's book is small and not easy to see clearly in detail. Moreover, certain details of the drawing have been blacked out.

The original relief comes from a tomb at the ancient Mayan ceremonial center of Palenque, Chiapas, Mexico. (It was found in 1952, not 1935, as von Däniken reports.*) It is carved on the lid of a sarcophagus buried under a large pyramid. The date of the burial (A.D. 683) can be determined by the accompanying Mayan glyphs.

Several of von Däniken's points about the relief can be re-examined with a clearer illustration.† The 'rocket' is pointed at the end, but there is something perched on top of it. If a child could identify the carving as a rocket, he could certainly identify the 'hood ornament' as a giant bird resembling a rooster! (Actually, this is a quetzal, the national bird of Guatemala.) Aerodynamically, the rooster-style hood ornament might have caused problems.

The 'spacecraft' is rather small, with few outer protections for the rider. Of greater concern is the fact that the astronaut has his head protruding *outside* the rocket. It is also strange that the figure is barefoot and does not wear gloves (both fingernails and toenails are illustrated) and has a complicated 'helmet' which does not cover his face. Except for a breechcloth and typical Mayan jade anklets, bracelets, and necklace, and the 'helmet' on his head, our astronaut is naked. In other words, he is a typically costumed upper-class Mayan of around A.D. 700 as pictured in other Mayan carvings and paintings.

* If the reader is interested in the exciting story of the discovery of the tomb, it may be found on pp. 296–97 in C. W. Ceram's *The March of Archaeology* (New York: Alfred A. Knopf, 1970), or in the article 'The Mystery of the Temple of the Inscriptions' in the March 1953 issue of *Archaeology* magazine, written by Alberto Ruz Lhuillier, the archaeologist who discovered the tomb.

† A comparison with von Däniken's own illustration was planned so that the reader could see the differences for himself, but permission to reprint his drawing was refused by von Däniken's English publisher, Souvenir Press of London.

The Palenque 'astronaut', carved on a sarcophagus lid from the Temple of Inscriptions, Palenque, Mexico. Although von Däniken sees a man piloting a rocket in this illustration, the personage is actually a deceased ruler, Pacal, in a state of suspension between two worlds – the world of the living and that of the dead. He is shown here in a composite design of a cross, a two-headed serpent, and a corn plant, rich in Mayan symbolism. *Drawing by Agustin Villagra. From The Civilization of the Ancient Maya by Alberto Ruz Lhuillier (1970). By permission of the Instituto Nacional de Antropologia e Historia, Córdoba, Mexico*

6

Around the inside of the tomb itself are other carvings of individuals with complicated headdresses, each representing a plant or animal native to the area that the Maya used for food or other purposes. One 'helmet' is a representation of a corn plant. Needless to say, this is not the sophisticated type of gear that our astronauts use. Although it might be a life-support system – the plant would produce oxygen to breathe and corn for food – it does not represent a technology that

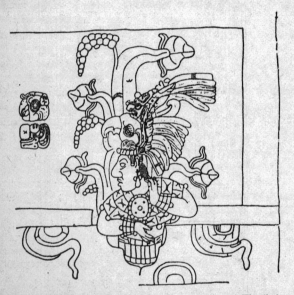

Bas-relief from the north side of Pacal's sarcophagus. The 'helmet' is apparently a representation of a corn plant. *From Anales, vol. 10 (1956), 'Exploraciones Arqueológicas en Palenque', by Alberto Ruz Lhuillier. By permission of the Instituto Nacional de Antropologia e Historia, Córdoba, Mexico*

we might reasonably expect astronaut-gods to depend on for space travel.

Inside the sarcophagus were found the bones of a man, with jade beads and ornaments on his ankles, wrists, and neck. A jade mosaic mask was over his face; contrary to von

Däniken's implication that all jade comes from China,[4] sources have been located in Mexico and North America.[5]

Study the illustration of the relief for yourself, while posing the question of whether or not the man and associated objects are ready for space travel. But do more than that. Put it in context. Look at other Mayan carvings and paintings, their buildings and their everyday possessions. Perhaps the complicated forms are not representations of spacemen, but are typical figures rendered in the ancient Mayan art style, which, like the Baroque style of seventeenth- and eighteenth-century Europe, filled all blank spaces with imaginative forms.

According to archaeologists who have thoroughly studied the glyphic evidence at the sacred site of Palenque, the Temple of the Inscriptions was a royal tomb, in the manner of the pyramids of Egypt. The personage buried inside was a king, and the Inscriptions tomb was a holy shrine erected in his honor. Alberto Ruz Lhuillier, the discoverer of the tomb, had this to say about its significance:

> This discovery demonstrated that the American pyramid was not necessarily and exclusively the solid substructure for a temple as has been thought up to date in contradistinction to the Egyptian pyramid. It revealed as well, a similar psychological attitude towards death on the part of the Pharaoh and the Palenque 'Halach Uinic' as well as a cultural parallelism inasmuch as the building of such monuments signified for both the Egyptians and the Maya an incredible waste of collective effort for the benefit of a privileged person.[6]

The name of the king and the details of his royal history are well established. Pacal, which is the Mayan word for shield, born in A.D. 603, was in power, at least by name, at the age of twelve years, 125 days (in A.D. 615), and died at the age of eighty years, 158 days, in A.D. 683.[7] Detailed translations of the hieroglyphics on the edge of the sarcophagus lid and other comprehensive information can be found in the two volumes of *Primera Mesa Redonda de Palenque: A Conference on the Art, Iconography, and Dynastic History of Palenque*, published in 1974.[8]

The scene carved on the stone slab covering Pacal's sarcophagus, thought by von Däniken to represent a spaceship, is not a technological illustration, but a religious one.

To appreciate the significance of this ritual scene, one must know something of the world view of the seventh-century Maya. Nature worship was the basis of their religion. The sun did not merely rise in the east; it was *reborn* each day and passed through the underworld each night. By germinating the corn plant, it gave the Mayan people life. The rain god was responsible for water, another necessity of life. To the Maya, 'the life cycle of the basic food plants interpreted as the passion and the resurrection of the deity represented a promise of immortality for man'.[9] The practice of burying the dead had a special religious significance: 'man [was] fated to return one day to earth . . . [as] the corn whose grain must be buried in order to germinate'.[10] The ancient Maya also believed in 'the divine essence of the king-priest and his power to intercede with the gods, on behalf of humanity, principally to insure the perpetuation of mankind through his own immortality'.[11]

The motivation was the same in the case of Pacal's burial. His subjects built the Temple of the Inscriptions as a prayer for the rebirth of their departed ruler. The religious symbolism inscribed on the tomb lid describes the scene. Pacal is facing upward, straight toward the zenith, where a quetzal takes its place as herald of the dawn and the rising of the sun god.* The plumed serpent bird, as the quetzal is also called, rests on the top of a cross, which represents the sacred maize tree (or corn plant). A similar cruciform motif can be seen in another scene from the Temple of the Cross. The rest of what von Däniken said 'any child would identify . . . as a rocket' consists of a two-headed serpent draped over the corn plant symbol, and some large corn leaves.

The Inscriptions tomb lid seems to be a composite art form, borrowing elements from these two tablets from

---

* When asked by the *Playboy* interviewer what the bird was doing on the front of the rocket, von Däniken said it might represent flight.

different temples. The quetzal is up at the top and the 'Earth Monster', or guardian of the underworld, at the base. What von Däniken calls a 'darting flame' representing the rocket's exhaust very likely represents the roots of the corn plant. The 'astronaut's' seat has been identified by archaeologists as Pacal's royal badge of rulership. According to Merle Greene Robertson, an authority on Mayan art, the representation of a corn plant is an important part of the badge. 'The ritual planting of corn is foremost in the minds of the Maya even today, and this was certainly so in the past. The corn plants, the new leaves, are the sign of rebirth – the answered prayer for immortality.'[12] In Pacal's case, the prayer for his rebirth is properly depicted as he is falling into the earth.

> The Earth Monster receives Pacal in the instant of death or suspension between worlds, and embellished on the head of the earth monster is the quadripartite badge, the most important single sign in the entire tomb, the sign which actually takes over part of the figure of the lord. What else would encompass and engulf the person of such royal status, important enough to have designated for his remains, the most splendid of all Maya tombs, than his inherited 'badge of Kings', proclaiming his rightful inheritance from possibly even the Sun God.[13]

10

Caves Filled with Gold

Some of the most sensational pieces of 'evidence' claimed by von Däniken for his astronaut-gods are the gold* treasures he says were discovered in a gigantic tunnel system under Ecuador and Peru. In *The Gold of the Gods* (1972) many examples of these treasures are illustrated. They were found in the churchyard of one Father Crespi, who according to von Däniken was given special permission by the Vatican to carry out his archaeological research. 'Today I know,' says von Däniken, 'that the biggest treasure from the dark tunnels is not on show in South American museums. It lies in the back patio of the Church of Maria Auxiliadora at Cuenca in Ecuador . . .'[1]

The subterranean tunnels are said to contain a fantastic 'zoo' of solid metal animal statues, seven chairs made of a strange material resembling plastic, and a library of two or three thousand metal plaques ' . . . which might contain a synopsis of the history of humanity, as well as an account of the origin of mankind on earth and information about a vanished civilization'.[2] The above statement von Däniken quotes from a document prepared by Juan Moricz, a South American explorer. In this document Moricz asks the Ecuadorian government to verify and assess the value of

* Von Däniken refers to these objects sometimes as metal, sometimes as gold.

87

some curious objects he found in a number of caves.

It was in March 1972 that von Däniken first met Moricz and claims to have been led on a personal tour through the mysterious underworld. Von Däniken begins *The Gold of the Gods* by saying: 'To me this is the most incredible, fantastic story of the century. It could easily have come straight from the realms of Science Fiction if I had not seen and photographed the incredible truth in person.'³ But when the German news magazine *Der Spiegel* dispatched a reporter to interview Juan Moricz for its 19 March 1973 issue, Moricz called von Däniken a liar. The following excerpts have been taken from that interview:

SPIEGEL: Mr Moricz, in his most recent book, Erich von Däniken claims to have descended with you into a secret cave world in Ecuador.

MORICZ: Däniken has never been in the caves – unless it was in a flying saucer.

SPIEGEL: He writes that you even showed him a pre-historic library of engraved metal folios, an entire zoo of golden animals, a cavern with chairs around a table.

MORICZ: If he claims to have seen the library and the other things himself then that's a lie. That's extremely indecent. We didn't show him these things. He even fudges with the photos; for example, the photo on page 15 of his *Aussat und Kosmos* [*The Gold of the Gods*] was taken on our expedition in 1969. It shows a cave entrance washed out by water. The amulet depicted on page 20 I did not find in a cave as he writes.

SPIEGEL: Why does Däniken make such claims?

MORICZ: I told him everything. For hours, for days, he squeezed it out of me. He wanted to hear more and more. He even hinted at $200,000 for a cave expedition.

SPIEGEL: Why did nothing come of that?

MORICZ: He didn't have the time. An expedition to the caves in eastern Ecuador would have taken at least fourteen days. But he was here only about a week.

SPIEGEL: So instead, you led him to a side entrance of the cave world, as Däniken calls it?

MORICZ: Yes, we drove with him in the Jeep to Cuenca for two days and showed him one of the many cave entrances in that area. But we could not enter this cave; it was blocked. Däniken can lie as much as he wants to, but not me . . .

SPIEGEL: In August of last year [1972] Däniken came to Ecuador again; for what purpose?

MORICZ: It was only a short visit, only two or three days. I think he came to say confession, but he didn't. Instead he invited my lawyer, Dr Peña Mattheus, and me to the book fair in Frankfurt for the presentation of his book – probably as self-justification. Mr Däniken probably took us for semi-savages who were too dumb to capitalize on their own knowledge.

SPIEGEL: Did you know then that Däniken was passing your tale off as his own experiences?

MORICZ: He didn't bring his book along. He only read us a few passages out of a galley proof. Däniken had promised that he would refer in his book only to my discoveries and a book that I myself plan to write. The caves really do exist, you know.

SPIEGEL: You claim that a tunnel system hundreds of kilometers long runs under the Andes from Ecuador to Peru and Bolivia . . .

MORICZ: . . . yes, from Cuzco, for example, the old imperial city of the Incas in Peru, the caves lead all the way to Bolivia, even to the sea.

SPIEGEL: Have you walked all of these caves?

MORICZ: No, but I've seen the entrances. I base my claims on mythology . . .

SPIEGEL: Were these tunnels created by natural means?

MORICZ: Many of these caves were formed by water erosion, but others were constructed . . .

SPIEGEL: An expedition could unveil the secret of the treasure. The Econ-Verlag [von Däniken's German publisher] has announced that it wants to send different scientists into the caves.

MORICZ: Econ has never written to me. Only Däniken has announced that he wants to come here in March on an expedition with a film team and scientists. Whether I participate will depend entirely on the conditions. It just won't do to ignite a discussion with lies and fan the flames with an expedition in order to profit more and more.[4]

Der Spiegel reported in an earlier issue that the geology professor Fritz Stibane of the University of Giessen examined caves in the area in question, but found no artificial tunnel systems and no gold treasures.[5] In the August 1974 *Playboy* interview, von Däniken acknowledged that Moricz had denied taking him into the caves and showing him the metal objects. But he held to his claim that he was in the caves with Moricz, although 'not at the main entrance'.[6]

But what about Father Crespi?

It is reported by *Der Spiegel* that others besides von Däniken have seen the Crespi treasure, and although there are some excellent pieces (pre-eminently the stone ones), the German source says, 'most were found to be imitations, made of tin and brass, like one can buy by the dozens in souvenir shops in Cuenca. The Danish archaeologist Olaf Holm, living in Ecuador, assured *Spiegel* that the old man, Padre Crespi, had difficulty distinguishing silver from tin, and brass from gold'.[7]

Another archaeologist, Pino Turolla of Miami, Florida, confirms this report and accuses von Däniken of writing a fraudulent book (*The Gold of the Gods*) with phony pictures. Turolla has, in fact, shown the *Miami News* his own photo of one of the 'artifacts' and revealed its origin. Turolla has seen the little factory clearing where, he says, the stuff is actually made by local Ecuadorian Indians. The natives then trade what is mostly junk to father Crespi for some clothes or small sums of money. Crespi, it turns out, is a much-loved but eccentric old man who collects this stuff, which according to the *Miami News* is 'closer to copper plumbing than God Gold'. Says Turolla, 'Once I recognized a copper toilet bowl float in Father Crespi's collection."[8]

The director of the Museo del Banco Central del Ecuador at Quito, Hernan Crespo, was equally outraged at von Däniken's cave story. The Ecuadorian government itself investigated a similar cave story four years ago and came away disappointed. The caves they checked out contained no gold – only *tayo* birds.[9]

11

Other Strange 'Evidence'

The Tiahuanaco Calendar

To von Däniken, archaeologists are hucksters and 'old
duffers' trying to pull the wool over the eyes of the mis-
informed public. He refers to 'tricks' by which 'scholars
could conjure [his evidence] . . . into the great mosaic of
accepted archaeological thinking'.[1] His attitude toward professional archaeologists and their methods (about which he
does not seem to be greatly familiar) is evident in the following discussion of Tiahuanaco, Bolivia:

> There is no plausible explanation for the beginning or the end of
> this culture. Of course, this does not stop some archaeologists
> from making the bold and self-confident assertion that the site of
> the ruins is 3,000 years old. They date this age from a couple of
> ridiculous little clay figures, which cannot possibly have any-
> thing in common with the age of the monolith. Scholars make
> things very easy for themselves. They stick a couple of old pots-
> herds together, search for one or two adjacent cultures, stick a
> label on the restored find and – hey, presto! – once again every-
> thing fits splendidly into the approved pattern of thought.[2]

Everyone is aware how car styles change every year or
so, and how obvious the contrast is between the Model-T
and the modern Fords. This type of stylistic change over
time is found in commonly used material items in all civilizations. Archaeologists study differences in style between

93

objects and the context or location of these objects, and then construct chronologies which tentatively date civilizations. Chronologies are so often constructed on the basis of potsherds because clay pottery containers were used in the majority of ancient civilizations for storing, preparing, serving, and eating food and liquids. Such everyday use indicates that pottery fragments will show a series of stylistic changes and will be readily discovered in excavations. In fact, broken pottery is the archaeologist's most common find. Hundreds of thousands of pieces are often excavated from one site. Most chronogolies based on stylistic change in pottery form and decoration have been substantiated by carbon-14 dating and other methods. These common items can be extremely useful to those studying about the time in which people lived and what they did.

Broken pottery was as much a part of the culture of Tiahuanaco, which built the monolithic Gate of the Sun, as aluminium cans or plastic plates are a part of our society. It is therefore a valid indicator of the age of this civilization.*

In relation to a find in Tiahuanaco, von Däniken presents us with some interpretations that might at first seem rather remarkable:

> ... what would people say if there were a calendar which gave the equinoxes, the astronomical seasons, the positions of the moon for every hour and also the movements of the moon, even taking the rotation of the earth into account?
>
> That is no mere hypothetical question. This calendar exists. It was found in the dry mud at Tiahuanaco. It is a disconcerting find. It yields irrefutable facts and proves – can our self-assurance admit such a proof? – that the beings who produced, devised, and used the calendar had a higher culture than ours.[3]

* If you want to see how archaeologists arrived at the date of approximately AD 800 (*not* three thousand years ago, as von Däniken says) for Tiahuanaco, consult such books as J. Alden Mason's *The Ancient Civilizations of Peru*, first published in 1957 (revised 1964) by Penguin Books; Gordon R. Willey's *An Introduction to American Archaeology, vol. 2, South America* (Englewoods Cliffs, N.J.: Prentice-Hall, 1971); E. P. Lanning's *Peru Before the Incas* (Englewoods Cliffs, N.J.: Prentice-Hall, 1967).

If this calendar exists, its whereabouts seems to be unknown. Von Däniken provides no reference to where we might find even a picture of this remarkable construction, nor a description of how it was supposed to have made such fine calculations. But then, equally frustrating are the references in von Däniken's books to platinum found in pre-Colombian Peru and aluminium in ancient China.[4] No original sources or museums are listed where these items can be located and checked.

Even if it turns out that such a calendar was used by the ancient people of Tiahuanaco, our self-assurance need not be threatened. Modern computers can do all the computations that von Däniken mentions, and more. In fact, we were able to do the computations before we traveled in space; so the people who devised the calendar in South America weren't necessarily spacemen. Furthermore, to determine such basic astronomical data is not exceedingly difficult.

Ancient agricultural peoples found it quite important to know when to plant, how long the growing seasons would be, when to expect the rainy season, and when to expect hot and cold weather. Long before the simple calendar was devised, the fact that the sun does not set at exactly the same point on the horizon each day could not have gone unnoticed. Although this shift is not readily apparent from one day to the next, the changing position of the sun becomes very conspicuous throughout the course of a year. Eventually, as the repeated pattern was observed, simple markers were probably erected to indicate positions. On the two equinoxes (approximately March 21 and September 23 of each year) the sun rises exactly in the direction of true east and sets exactly in the west. The two solstice points (occurring about June 21 and December 21) represent the rising and setting of the sun at points farthest away from true east and true west.

The rising and setting positions of the moon, although more complicated, were probably noticed as well. The stones of Stonehenge, which is believed to have been constructed around 1500 B.C., seem to mark the moon cycle as well as that of the sun; this ancient site may well have served as a giant calendar to mark the seasons. Rock paintings and engravings on a mammoth tusk from the Ice Age seem to indicate that prehistoric man recorded the pattern of the phases of the moon.

No, the Tiahuanaco calendar, which we know only from von Däniken's description, is not a 'disconcerting find'.

The Olmec Sculptures

Among the giant stoneworks von Däniken tells us about are the incredible sculptures of the Olmecs. 'With their beautifully helmeted giant skulls,' he says, 'they can be admired only on the sites where they were found, for they will never be on show in a museum. No bridge in the country [Mexico] could stand their weight.'[5] Perhaps von Dâniken is not aware that three of them are now on display in Mexico City, and there is one also in Explorers Hall at the National Geographic Society in Washington, D.C.[6]

The 'Great God Mars' from Tassili

Embossed into the cover of the G. P. Putnam hard-bound edition of *Chariots of the Gods?* is a representation of a Tassili fresco von Däniken calls the 'great god Mars'.[7] The figure in the rock painting is Jabbaren (*le grand dieu martien*), so named by its discoverer, the French archaeologist Henri Lhote.

The figure does look something like a man in a spacesuit. But that's not what it is. It is one example of an artistic tradition appropriately called the 'Period of the Round Heads', which can be traced through its various phases and subphases of development.[8] This particular rock painting, which dates to around 6000 B.C., is one of many that are found in the same region. Several other paintings illustrated in Henri Lhote's book *The Search for the Tassili Frescoes*[9] show similar round-headed female figures with pointy pendulous breasts. (Were these perhaps female astronauts?) Other subjects included elephants, giraffes, wild oxen, lions, ostriches, and warthogs. As for the 'Martian god' himself, he is quite likely an ordinary human being wearing a ritual mask and costume. Henri Lhote seemed to be quite sure of this: 'This typical mask revealed, in unexpected fashion, though without any sort of doubt, that Negroes, in past ages, really had inhabited the Sahara, and also that in neolithic times masks had played there the same role that they do today in the animistic cults of the primitive societies in West Africa'.[10]

More Rock Paintings

In *Gods from Outer Space*, a picture caption states that the headgear worn by what appears to be a dancing figure in a prehistoric painting from Val Camonica, Italy, 'looks very much like some kind of aerial'.[11] However, it takes far less imagination to recognize in this picture a pair of deer antlers! A ceremonial costume is also quite obvious.

The caption on the next page says that 'So far no one has given a plausible explanation of these complicated rock paintings from Santa Barbara in California.'[12] The same illustration appeared in the *National Enquirer* on 24 December 1974, and was associated with the front-page headline: '1ST EVIDENCE THAT BEINGS FROM OUTER SPACE HAVE VISITED U.S.' The accompanying article explained that a Swiss electronics engineer by the name of Heinrich Gosswiler 'recognized' the Santa Barbara rock painting as a complex scientific diagram. The *Enquirer* quoted Gosswiler as saying: 'It appears to be a blueprint for artificially inducing the elements of life.'[13] Of course, von Däniken's picture was displayed at the top of the page on which the article appeared and reference was made to his book *Gods from Outer Space*.

But while Gosswiler may think the rock painting represents a scientific diagram, the Quechan Indians of southern California have quite different ideas.[14] The hieroglyphics carved into the rocks by the Quechans' ancestors had a simple, but vital, purpose. The various arrows, circles, wavy lines, and stars were symbols designed to convey important messages, not between man and outer-space beings but between one hunting party and another. Sometimes they were instructions on how to find the nearest water hole, or a warning that there were Gila monsters in the area. A circle usually symbolized the camp, and the lines indicate paths taken from home. A zigzag line tells that the party had a difficult time along some particular path, and various other petroglyphs give the details of the story. The Quechan explanation of the rock paintings seems to make more sense, in the context in which the petroglyphs are found, than the theories of Gosswiler and von Däniken.

The Rustproof Iron Pillar

In *Chariots of the Gods?* von Däniken tells us: 'In the courtyard of a temple in Delhi there exists ... a column made of welded iron parts that has been exposed to weathering for more than 4,000 years without showing a trace of rust. In addition it is unaffected by sulphur or phosphorus. Here we have an unknown alloy from antiquity staring us in the face.'[15] What is amazing here is not the special properties of the iron pillar, but how von Däniken could make four errors in only three sentences.

First of all, the Iron Pillar of Meharauli is not actually *in* Delhi but nearby. Secondly, it is not four thousand, but approximately fifteen hundred years old. Thirdly, it is not made of 'welded ... parts'; it is actually a single piece of iron. And fourthly, it is not an 'unknown alloy', but rather pure iron.

Von Däniken did, however get one thing right. The iron column is virtually rustproof. According to A. L. Basham, in *The Wonder That Was India*,[16] it was purposely made that way, to serve as a lasting shrine to a king (probably Chandra Gupta II) who died near the beginning of the fifth century. What prevents the pillar from rusting, he says, is in fact the great purity of the metal. The process of rusting (or oxidation) requires a catalyst. One was not present in this case, since the iron is almost chemically pure. And although the ancient Indian metallurgists were indeed far advanced for their time, a good European iron founder of about one hundred years ago could have produced the same result. The job need not, therefore, be attributed to an outer-space technology.

Von Däniken finally admitted this, incidentally, in his interview for *Playboy* magazine. He said, ' . . . when I wrote *Chariots of the Gods?* the information I had concerning this iron column was as I presented it. Since then, I have found that investigations were made and they came to quite different results, so we can forget about this iron thing.'[17]

Elephantine Island

'The Island of Elephantine,' says von Däniken, ' . . . is called Elephantine even in the oldest texts, because it was supposed to resemble an elephant'.[18] Conclusion: the island must have been observed from the air in ancient times. What other explanation could there be for an island's being named for an elephant?

In the first place, the island was originally called *Yeb* or *Yebu*, in Egyptian, because of the ivory that was sold there; it has also been suggested that elephants did once occupy the island.[19] Similarly, the later name, Elephantine, is deriver from the Greek word *elephantinos*, meaning 'ivory'[20] In the second place, this small parcel of land in the Nile is not at all shaped like an elephant, as can be seen in the map of Elephantine Island.

12

Extraterrestrial Science?

As we have now seen, without denying the possibility of von Däniken's thesis, archaeologists have offered so many more plausible and more substantial explanations for man's physical and cultural development that there is really no reason to bring extraterrestrial 'gods' into the picture. In this chapter I will try to show that the 'evidence' claimed by von Däniken to represent the science and technology of the ancient gods falls far short of what might be expected from an advanced race of beings capable of interstellar space travel. Moreover, much, if not all, of the scientific knowledge and technology von Däniken claims for them and speculates upon seems remarkably close to developments in our own recent past and our aspirations for the future. What an astounding coincidence! It's as astounding as the 'coincidence' that the materials going into science fiction are derived from human imagination and experience.

It will be instructive to take a look at a theme from science fiction similar to von Däniken's – the intervention of advanced extraterrestrials in the lives of the early man-apes of earth. In 1950 there appeared a short story by Arthur C. Clarke entitled 'The Sentinel'. In it, an extraterrestrial artifact was discovered on the moon by earth astronauts. What made the discovery such a powerful case of 'future shock' was not just its otherworldly origin, but its age: *four million years*. This meant that long before human development was under way, other beings of a very high order of intelligence had been winging their way across the cosmos.

Clarke's story later provided the basic idea for *2001: A Space Odyssey*, the Academy Award-winning motion picture that pushed the boundaries of the popular imagination to new limits.

It was, in effect, a space-age Genesis; a creation story featuring mankind as the product of a cosmic experiment being carried out, not by the traditional Judeo-Christian God, but by extraterrestrial intelligences who, because of attributes acquired during their own long evolution, might themselves be defined as gods. In other words, the motion picture *2001* and the novel based on the screenplay contained the essential elements of the ancient astronaut theory prior to the fame of von Däniken. Moreover, the artifact in the story was more than a piece of evidence proving the existence of intelligent life beyond the earth. In *2001*, the artifact was a black monolith, a vertically standing slab resembling a tombstone, which had been deliberately buried on the moon four million years before. When the monolith was excavated (after having been discovered because of its magnetic properties) and then exposed to the sunlight, it would serve as a signal to the intelligences that put it there. In this way, the 'sentinel' would beam the message that man had reached a new step in his evolution – the capability of leaving the earth and venturing into the cosmos.

In the novel version of *2001*, Arthur Clarke tells of the monolith's crystalline counterpart, used as a teaching machine for the man-apes back on earth. It was, in effect, a highly complicated computer that thoroughly probed and mapped the brains and bodies of the early hominids, studied their reactions, evaluated their potential, and gave them 'human' intelligence. Stanley Kubrick, the film maker who made this classic famous, told *Playboy* magazine in 1968: 'I will say that the God concept is at the heart of *2001* – but not any traditional, anthropomorphic image of God. I don't believe in any of Earth's monotheistic religions, but I do believe that one can construct an intriguing *scientific* definition of God."¹ And so this is what he did.

But Clarke and Kubrick gave their 'gods' a much higher level of technology than von Däniken gave his. They were not at all of a human form. Indeed, having freed themselves from matter, they existed as pure energy. Even the earth people of *2001* that evolved from ape-man were far more advanced than von Däniken's ancient astronauts. They had talking and thinking computers an enormous space station, full-scale colonization of the moon, and artificially induced hibernation for long space journeys. No evidence of this kind of technology has been found as testimony to the presence of ancient astronauts, although von Däniken thinks otherwise. He cites Egyptian mummification techniques as evidence for advanced scientific practices in the ancient past. Mummification, he says, was a way to preserve bodies until the gods came back from outer space and awakened them to a new life. (He compares this technique to Robert C. W. Ettinger's concept of preserving bodies in deep freeze and defrosting them when the diseases from which they died are curable.) This would be an interesting speculation if it were not for a few details of the Egyptian practice of mummification.

The first thing Egyptian priests did to prepare a corpse for mummification was to pull its brain out through its nose with a pair of long copper tweezers. Then the empty cranial cavity was filled with hot liquid resin. After this, the viscera (heart, lungs, stomach, liver, etc.) were extracted and placed in four Canopic jars or wrapped in four packages, which were placed inside the body. Finally, the body was soaked in a gluey substance consisting principally of resins. Moreover, the process of reawakening would be difficult even for 'gods'. To extract the mummy of Tutankhamen from his coffin, for example, it had to be heated to 932 degrees F. to melt the solidified embalming fluid. And in another case, the wrappings of the mummy of Pum II had to be removed with hammer and chisel and a Stryker saw.²

If the 'gods' used techniques such as these to produce hibernation for long space voyages, it is difficult to imagine how they ever got to earth in the first place. Mummification practices obviously do not qualify as advanced extraterrestrial science.

'Today, in the twentieth century,' writes von Däniken, 'no architect could build a copy of the pyramid of Cheops, even if the technical resources of every continent were at his disposal.'[3] He certainly underestimates our present abilities as well as those of our ancestors. As we saw in previous chapters, the great stones of the pyramids, Olmec heads, and Easter Island statues could be transported and raised by relatively simple mechanical means and the toil of large numbers of workmen. Today, should we want to embark on such a project, we could substitute jackhammers for stone hammers, hydraulic trucks for sledges.

An example that von Däniken gives of a 'technical invention' of space people is none other than the Ark of the Covenant, which God told Moses how to construct. Von Däniken thinks it might have been a kind of radio set used for 'communication between Moses and the spaceship',[4] and he seems to recall that 'Moses made use of this "transmitter" whenever he needed help and advice'.[5] It's hard to see how this crude 'condenser' made of wood and gold with a gold cherub serving as a magnet could represent the technology of a superadvanced race of extraterrestrials.

Von Däniken was not the first to suggest that the Ark of the Covenant was an electric condenser. The idea was presented by Robert Charroux in his *One hundred Thousand Years of Man's Unknown History* (1963), and he in turn attributes it to Maurice Denis-Papin, author of *Cours Élémentaire d'Électricité générale*, published in 1948. Charroux also speculates that the Ark might have contained batteries similar to those on display in the Baghdad Museum.

Von Däniken refers to the Baghdad batteries as if they were indeed the products of an advanced alien technology. The first of these objects was found on 14 June 1936, by the

Iraq State Railways Department while in the course of earth-moving operations outside Baghdad. About a dozen others have been found nearby in archaeological sites representative of the Parthian period (248 B.C to A.D. 226). If they are really batteries, then they would be the most primitive form of simple cell possible. A typical unit is composed of an ovoid pottery jar (eighteen by nine centimeters) with a copper cylinder, an iron rod, and some bitumen crumbs. A replica was tested in 1960 by John B. Pierczynski of the University of North Carolina. Using an electrolyte of 5 percent vinegar solution, one-half volt of electricity was obtained from the cell, which lasted eighteen days. The most likely purpose for such a battery would be in a primitive electroplating process; one-half volt would be a sufficient electrical potential to electroplate silver onto copper.[6] I cannot see how these batteries would have been particularly beneficial to ancient space voyagers.

Early in *Chariots of the Gods?* von Däniken describes an imaginary journey of a spaceship and its landing on a planet similar to earth. After creating a new race and leaving it to evolve to greater heights, astronauts would depart, but 'would leave behind clear and visible signs which only a highly technical, mathematically based society would be able to understand much, much later'. But after the visitors have gone, the still primitive people will make the episode into a saga and turn the 'presents and implements and everything that the space travelers left behind into holy relics'.[7]

Where are the visible signs to be interpreted later by advanced cultures? Certainly they are not the batteries and radio sets just described. The early space travelers do not seem to have left us anything like the *Pioneer 10* plaque designed by Cornell astronomers Carl Sagan and Frank Drake to inform other intelligent life of our existence, appearance, and location in the universe. This plaque was made of a complex alloy that could have been produced only by a relatively advanced technology.

The opening sequence of the television special 'In Search of Ancient Astronauts' (NBC-TV, 5 January 1973) depicts

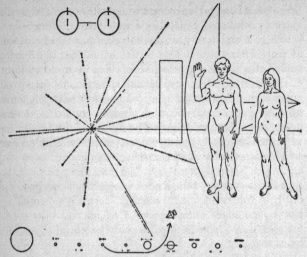

The Pioneer 10 plaque: an artifact from earth.

a few New Guinea natives sitting forlornly on top of a hill beside their clumsy imitations of airplanes and control towers. They are waiting, the audience is told, for the Americans who had come in large planes (during World War II) to return. The implication was obvious. If the New Guinea natives would make representations of us, so our ancestors would have made drawings and statues of spacemen. The drawings von Däniken calls to our attention are the ones found at Tassili in the Sahara that show beings supposedly in bulky suits with helmets and antennae.

But the thought that arises on viewing the New Guinea scene is this. If you were to walk down the hill on which the natives were sitting and look around the countryside, you would surely find remains of planes, runways, control towers, barracks, etc., all rusted and broken. Whole complexes of a technology obviously beyond the New Guinea peoples of the 1940s would still be there, even down to the cans that once contained C rations.

It seems curious in the light of the debris we left in the

South Pacific and on the moon that not one of von Däniken's 'finds' is undoubtedly made by extraterrestrial beings.

In his *Playboy* interview, von Däniken was asked how the ancient astronauts could have 'walked all over the Earth, altered the course of human history and departed without leaving a trace'. Sidestepping the question, he spoke of monuments, allowing that the visitors might have left some sort of monitoring device (an apparant reference to the monolith in *2001*) that we just haven't found. It would be well hidden so a technically advanced people wouldn't come upon it and 'take it apart with a screwdriver'.[8]

13

The Mysterious Moons of Mars

The moons of Mars are not as famous as the 'canals', but they have been equally intriguing to those who have seriously studied them. They have also attracted the attention of many unorthodox writers including von Däniken, who suggested that the astronaut-gods might have come from Mars.

These anomalies – the canals, which have been thought to be artificial constructions for the purpose of irrigating a dying, arid world, and the mysterious moons, unlike any other known natural satellites in the solar system – constitute the basis for the theory of intelligent life on Mars.

Both the canals and the moons were discovered in 1877 during a favorable opposition (a time when Mars is at its closest approach to earth). An Italian astronomer, Giovanni Schiaparelli, using an eight-and-three-quarter-inch refracting telescope, saw some linear streaks crisscrossing the lighter areas of the planet. He called these markings *canali*, meaning 'channels', but the word was mis-translated into English, and they came to be known as the famous 'canals' of Mars. Asaph Hall, an American astronomer observing with the twenty-six-inch refractor of the U.S. Naval Observatory near Washington, D.C., while not able to see any 'canals', even with the larger instrument, did discover two tiny satellites orbiting Mars.

The idea that the canals were artificial was developed by Percival Lowell, who founded the now famous Lowell Observatory at Flagstaff, Arizona, in 1894. This was the year that H. G. Wells wrote his science fiction classic *The War of the Worlds*, in which beings from Mars invaded the earth. The accounts of Martian life given by Wells and Lowell were strikingly similar in certain respects, even though one was writing fiction and the other expounding a serious hypothesis.

Both writers described a dying planet on which the inhabitants composed one civilization joined together for the common purpose of survival. They also considered Mars to be a much older world than earth; hence evolutionary developments there must have been more advanced, especially with respect to intelligent life.

In the year immediately preceding the publication of Wells' Martian tale, Schiaparelli concluded that the *canali* were channels carrying water, although not necessarily designed and built by intelligent beings. Furthermore, he sometimes saw the canals as double lines, usually during the melting of the Martian polar caps. A single canal would change its appearance quite suddenly at this time and become two parallel lines running along the path formerly traversed by the one. Schiaparelli was so amazed by this that he at first suspected himself to be the victim of an optical illusion, but when he observed Mars again at another opposition, he saw the event repeated and was able to count twenty such canals that had doubled.

Lowell also observed the doubling phenomenon and theorized that the Martian canals were part of a gigantic irrigation system distributing water from the melting polar caps to the rest of the planet. He attributed his ability to see the canals (which were not reported by many other astronomers) to his astuteness as an observer and to the superior atmospheric conditions in Arizona. At one point, the professor was able to map 183 individual canals, 116 more than Schiaparelli had seen. He estimated their width to be between two and three miles for some and twenty-five and thirty miles for others. Their length was even more phenomenal; many exceeded 2,500 miles, and one was recorded as 3,540 miles long. Two thousand miles was common.

No natural theory could explain the canals, he felt. They could not be rivers because of their straightness, and not cracks, because then they would be bigger at one end and smaller at the other. He realized that an artificial canal up to thirty miles wide is rather large, even for a technologically advanced civilization, and reasoned that the lines were not the canals proper, but vegetation growing alongside. There were also round spots at the junctions of the canals – just where you would expect 'oases' to be found – that darkened seasonally, indicating the growth of vegetation.

But Mars was not the only planet on which Lowell could observe striking surface features. He also made drawings showing linear streaks on Mercury, Venus, and the satellites of Jupiter. One is therefore led to suspect exaggeration (to use a kind expression) as an ingredient in all of Lowell's plentary maps. Patrick Moore remarks in his *Guide to the Planets*: '[Lowell's] chart of Venus can only be described as fantastic; the features shown simply do not exist.'

Opposing Lowell in the canal controversy were astronomers who claimed that such features could be resolved with large telescopes in moments of excellent 'seeing'* into irregular spots and patches. To them, the canals were just a kind of optical effect which occurs when the human eye strains to see fine detail at the limits of visibility. It is well known that the eye tends to connect adjacent areas in a perceptual field and see them as lines.

This interpretation of the Martian canals does hold true in some cases, but in the majority of instances, the Lowellian lines have no relation to features of the Martian surface. NASA's *Mariner 9* photographic mission showed grooves or

---

* The image of Mars is frequently distorted by air currents in the earth's atmosphere, a condition referred to by astronomers as 'bad seeing'. Under bad seeing conditions, one may see less planetary detail – believe it or not – with a thirty-six-inch telescope than with a six-inch instrument.

rifts, such as the one corresponding to the large Coprates *canale*, but there were no signs of artificial canals, even though the entire surface of the planet was carefully mapped down to one kilometer (0.62 mile) resolution.[2] These close-up pictures are approximately one hundred times more revealing than the finest observations ever made with earth-bound telescopes.

The first strange thing usually mentioned about the Martian moons is their apparent prediction by Jonathan Swift in *Gulliver's Travels*, published in 1726. In the quotation that follows, Swift is referring to the Laputian astronomers, who have charge of the loadstone which guides an imaginary floating island.

> This Load-stone is under the Care of certain Astronomers, who from Time to Time give it such Positions as the Monarch directs. They spend the greatest Part of their Lives in observing the celestial Bodies, which they do by the Assistance of Glasses, far excelling ours in Goodness. For, although their largest Telescopes do not exceed three Feet, they magnify much more than those of a Hundred with us, and shew the Stars with greater Clearness. This Advantage hath enabled them to extend their Discoveries much farther than our Astronomers in *Europe*. They have made a Catalogue of ten Thousand fixed Stars, whereas the largest of ours do not contain about one third Part of that Number. They have likewise discovered two lesser Stars, or *Satellites*, which revolve about *Mars*; whereof the innermost is distant from the Center of the primary Planet exactly three of his Diameters, and the outermost five; the former revolves in the Space of ten Hours, and the latter in Twenty-one and a Half; so that the Squares of their periodical Times are very near in the same Proportion with the Cubes of their Distance from the Center of *Mars*, which evidently shews them to be governed by the same Law of Gravitation, that influences the other heavenly Bodies.[3]

This prophecy has turned out to be not too far from the truth; hence the many speculations as to how the moons of Mars could be described with such accuracy 150 years before their actual discovery.

But it is really not so strange that Mars was given two

moons. I. S. Shklovskii reminds us that 'Pythagorean ideas about the harmony of numbers were widely accepted in those days.'[4] The earth had one moon, they knew, and Jupiter was thought to have four (it actually has fourteen). Assuming a geometrical progression, it would be natural to pick two for the number of Martian moons. In fact, this is precisely what Johannes Kepler did in his speculations published under the title *Narratio de Jovis Satellitibus* in the year 1610.

Swift's statement of the relationship between the moons' periods of revolution and their distances from the center of Mars is also not surprising. Kepler's third law, which was first published in 1619, states that the square of the orbital period of a planet is proportional to the cube of its mean distance from the sun. Swift apparently made use of it. His actual figures for the moons' distances from Mars and their periods of revolution are not, of course, exact.

The two moons of Mars were again observed fictionally well before their actual discovery, this time by a visitor to our solar system in Voltaire's story 'Micromegas', published in 1752. He, like Swift, must have been aware of Kepler's work.

Immanuel Velikovsky, in his best-selling book *Worlds in Collision*, gave the opinion that Swift obtained his information from ancient manuscripts which described actual observations of the moons when Mars was close to the earth. Supposedly this is why Homer spoke of the 'two steeds of Mars' that drew his chariot.[5] One of Velikovsky's supporters, an astrologer by the name of Joseph F. Goodavage, makes the following statements in *Astrology: The Space Age Science* (1966): 'Mars *must* have come terrifyingly close to the earth in those days – close enough perhaps for men to have seen its so-called "moons". I say "so-called" because these two moons are not natural satellites.' In fact, Goodavage entitled the portion of his book from which this quote was taken 'The Satellite Cities Orbiting Mars'.[6] However, the original suggestion that the two moons were artificial satellites put into orbit by Martians was made, I believe, by

113

Gerald Heard, writing in 1950 about flying saucers.[7]

Von Däniken latched onto the idea of the moons' artificiality to support his claim that space travelers came to earth in ancient times. If a comet had crashed into Mars as Velikovsky said, he reasoned, some Martian giants could have escaped to earth and bred with the pre-humans they encountered.

The moons of Mars are in fact unusual, as von Däniken and others have pointed out. They are extremely small compared to the other known natural satellites in the solar system. (Their diameters have been estimated at ten miles for Phobos and five miles for Deimos.) Their orbits are relatively close in to Mars. Phobos orbits Mars about three times as fast as the planet itself rotates; no other known natural satellite has a period of revolution less than that of the body it orbits.

To help substantiate the artificial-satellite theory, von Däniken tells us in *Chariots of the Gods?* that 'Russian scientist I. S. Shklovskii and renowned American astronomer Carl Sagan, in their book *Intelligent Life in the Universe*, published in 1966, accept that the moon Phobos is an artificial satellite. As a result of a series of measurements, Sagan came to the conclusion that Phobos must be hollow and a hollow moon cannot be natural.'[8] Sagan denies this. 'This is one of several places where von Däniken misquotes me,' he says. 'As can clearly be seen by anyone who reads Chapter 26 of *Intelligent Life in the Universe* . . . it is Shklovskii and not I who proposed this idea; and even by 1966 both Shklovskii and I thought that the idea had little merit.'[9] Von Däniken has admitted the error but blames it on the translation of his book. 'I should have said "suggest",' he told his *Playboy* interviewer. 'In the German version, it says they "say yes" to the theory.'[10]

What 'measurements' were behind Shklovskii's speculation? They were observations of Phobos's orbital velocity made by the American astronomer B. P. Sharpless in 1945 and compared with earlier ones. This comparison seemed to indicate that Phobos was traveling faster and at the same time moving closer in to Mars. Shklovskii, looking for reasons for this reported acceleration of Phobos, considered atmospheric drag. (Resistance of the Martian atmosphere would cause the satellite's orbit to shrink, but the net result would be acceleration.) However, for atmospheric drag to be a factor, the density of Phobos would have to be very low for its size. Such a low density would be possible only if Phobos were hollow and therefore an artificial satellite.

In holding to the artificial-satellite theory to explain the moons of Mars, von Däniken states in *Chariots* that the theory of 'planetoids', or the theory that the moons are captured asteroids, as planetoids are now called, is 'untenable'.[11] Since he penned these lines, however, there have been some developments.

On 26 and 29 November 1971, *Mariner 9* obtained the first close-up photographs of any natural satellites in the solar system other than the earth's own moon. Phobos was revealed as a potato-shaped rock about sixteen miles long and thirteen miles wide, covered with craters. Deimos was also confirmed to be irregularly shaped, about eight miles across, and with a rough surface, cratered close to saturation.[12] Astronomers now think that the satellites are probably as old as the solar system itself and that 'both Phobos and Deimos appear to be the remnants of a larger body (or bodies) evolved through a complex collisional natural selection. Their appearance may be typical of many asteroids and other small solar system objects.'[13] So it seems that the artificial-satellite theory is not quite as promising as von Däniken thought.

14

'Gods' in Recent Times

> . . . we men, the creatures who inhabit this earth, must be to them
> [the Martians] at least as alien and lowly as are the monkeys and
> lemurs to us. The intellectual side of man already admits that life
> is an incessant struggle for existence, and it would seem that this
> too is the belief of the minds upon Mars. . . .
>
> The Tasmanians, in spite of their human likeness, were entirely
> swept out of existence in a war of extermination waged by
> European immigrants, in the space of fifty years. Are we such
> apostles of mercy as to complain if the Martians warred in the
> same spirit?
>
> H. G. WELLS, *The War of the Worlds*

For these ideas to be contained in Wells's novel, published in 1898, was one thing, but to be coming over the
American airwaves in the year 1938 was quite another. With
the Fascism of Mussolini and Hitler as a threat to world
peace, American fear was at an all-time high. So on the
night before Halloween, 30 October 1938, when Orson
Welles presented his radio play of H. G. Wells's *The War of
the Worlds*, approximately one million people believed that
the invasion was actually taking place, in spite of the fact
that the play began with the following introduction: 'The
Columbia Broadcasting System and its affiliated stations

present Orson Welles and the Mercury Theatre on the Air in "The War of the Worlds" by H. G. Wells.' Three additional announcements made during the program stated that the play was fiction. Furthermore, the program was listed in newspaper radio schedules: 'Today: 8.00–9.00 – play: H. G. Wells's "War of the Worlds" – WABC.'

People who feared that the earth was being attacked by Martians obviously did not take the time to check the authenticity of the information they had received, and proceeded to flee from their homes, or at least to close their windows to shut out the poison gas. As Martin Gardner remarks in his book *Fads & Fallacies in the Name of Science*: 'If . . . an invasion from Mars [could be] taken seriously in 1938, perhaps it is not so hard to understand a widespread acceptance of the spaceship theory of flying saucers in a decade that has split the atom . . .'[2]

The first reports of U.F.O.s (or unidentified flying objects) in what we might call modern times were of the 'foo-fighters' seen toward the end of World War II in Europe and in the western Pacific. These objects were reported as gold, red, or white balls of light, seemingly only two or three feet in diameter. They would appear alone or in groups, and reportedly 'played games' with the military pilots who spotted them. They would never attack the planes, but rather exhibited 'curiosity', and would follow and 'tease' the pilots.

'Flying saucer' was a press term coined in 1947 after Kenneth Arnold, piloting his private plane near Mount Ranier, Washington, reported seeing nine bright objects that 'flew like a saucer would if you skipped it across the water'. He also said of the objects (which some investigators believed could easily have been a formation of U.S. Air Force planes flying in the vicinity) that they 'made a tremendous impression on me . . . how they fluttered and sailed, tipping their wings alternately and emitting those very bright blue-white flashes from their surfaces. At the time I did not get the impression that these flashes were emitted by them, but rather that it was the sun's reflection from the extremely highly polished surface of their wings.'[3] Arnold then fell into the company of science fiction writer-editor Ray Palmer. In the spring of 1948, Arnold's first article appeared in Palmer's brand-new magazine, *Fate*.[4] The inevitable soon happened. A professional writer with a flair for the sensational, Donald Keyhoe, came onto the scene. With a highly popular article in *True* magazine entitled 'The Flying Saucers Are Real', which was hastily expanded into a book by the same name,[5] the flying saucer *business* began. As one U.F.O. investigator observed, 'By 1950 magazine and book publishers had discovered that money could be made in the U.F.O. field.'[6]

Keyhoe took up Arnold's suspicion that the military knew what the objects were and claimed that the U.S. Air Force was withholding information from the public. The Air Force, concerned that the sightings might have been of a new Russian weapon, did look into the matter, but denied there was anything to it. According to Captain Edward J. Ruppelt, who headed Project Blue Book:

> . . . The Air Force wasn't trying to cover up. It was just that they didn't want Keyhoe or any other saucer fans in their hair. . . . They didn't believe in flying saucers and couldn't feature anybody else believing. . . . The Air Force had a plan. . . . It called for a general officer to hold a short press conference, flash his stars, and speak the magic words 'hoaxes, hallucinations, and the misidentification of known objects'. *True*, Keyhoe and the rest would go broke trying to peddle their magazines. The *True* article did come out, the general spoke, the public laughed, and Keyhoe and *True* got rich.[7]

People wanted to know why the saucers were here, and Keyhoe was not lacking in suggestions. The alien spacemen could be concerned about our atomic explosions, he said, either because they feared an invasion by us when we achieved a practical means of space travel or because they were planning an 'exodus from space' themselves with intentions of colonizing the earth.[8] These ideas helped to create an uneasy feeling among a great many people who were already concerned about the atomic bomb. The fate of Hiroshima and Nagasaki made it quite clear that the human race could not survive another world war. Obviously the world needed saving. As it turned out, hope was not far away – no farther than the chosen few who were the 'contactees' of our benevolent 'Space Brothers' with whom we share the solar system.

The Space Brothers came from Venus, Mars, Jupiter, Saturn, Neptune, 'Clarion', and even from the earth in times gone by. The contactee stories were deeply rooted in a strong religious tradition. References were made to 'cosmic guidance' and 'new age thought' by our Space Brothers to warn and aid mankind in its folly. Then, too, in the classic manner of all shamanistic traditions, the contactees *alone* were in communication with the new gods of the sky. The special group of earthlings who were contacted represented the chosen few who received the call. This meant, of course, that organizations should be formed, publications printed and sold, lecture tours and TV appearances arranged, and other forms of commercialization brought into play.

If important messages were to be given for the benefit of all mankind, they would be received first (only by the contactees, of course) by means of mental telepathy or as 'voices inside the head'. This latter claim I have no reason to doubt. The connection between spiritualism and the new U.F.O. cults is pointed out by Robert S. Ellwood, a specialist in modern religions and a professor at the University of Southern California's School of Religion: 'The wise ones . . . come from a futuristic technology. Both types of groups employ the same manner of communication: vision and marvelous journeys, trance speaking and writing, seance circles and telepathy. The close interaction between Spiritualism and U.F.O. cults is not surprising, for one finds there is much exchange of persons between them.'[9]

Another characteristic of the contactees is that they have a very limited education or one dominated by techno-mechanical knowledge. This fact links the phenomenon to technological worship and accounts for the extreme naïveté of the stories that have been told.

By far the most famous of all the contactees and the

most successful in terms of book sales as well was George Adamski, who died in 1965. Prior to his alleged contact experiences, of which there were many, he earned his living by teaching 'esoteric philosophy' and by selling his photographs of flying saucers for seventy-five cents each. It is interesting that the 'ancient laws' which constituted a part of his teachings turned up later as messages given to him by the Space Brothers.

The first contact experiences claimed by Adamski occurred on 20 November 1952, on the California desert, 10.2 miles from Desert Center, toward Parker, Arizona. This precise location, plus about twenty pages of detailed description of a brief encounter with a man from Venus and his spacecraft, is given in Adamski's book *Flying Saucers Have Landed.*[10] His Venusian turns out to be a beardless, suntanned version of Jesus, wearing a ski suit and sandals. Adamski writes: 'The beauty of his form surpassed anything I had ever seen. And the pleasantness of his face freed me of all thought of my personal self. I felt like a child in the presence of one with great wisdom and much love, and I became very humble within myself . . . for from him was radiating a feeling of infinite understanding and kindness, with supreme humility.'[11]

Through a combination of gestures, facial expressions, and mental telepathy, the following was established: (1) The purpose of the Venusians' visit to earth; namely, their concern over our atomic bombs. (To express the concept of atomic explosions, the spaceman made gestures with his hands illustrating the cloud formations of the bombs and added the words 'Boom! Boom!')[12] (2) The existence of God as the 'Creator of All' was confirmed, as well as the immortality of the soul and reincarnation. Adamski's initial contact story ends with his walking the Venusian back to the flying saucer which was hovering nearby. A description of the craft is given in full detail, including theories of its operation and method of propulsion. Later contacts were to follow, supplemented with rides into space and lengthy dialogues with spacemen, whom he quoted verbatim in his second book, *Inside the Space Ships*.[13]

The 'literary' connection between ancient astronauts and modern 'UFOnauts' can be traced back to Adamski's first book, *Flying Saucers Have Landed*, published in 1953. It was co-written by Desmond Leslie, an electronics expert, talented writer, and devotee of the occult. The saucers came from the planet Venus, according to Leslie, and first landed on earth in exactly 18,617,841 B.C., 'when something resembling a man had evolved . . .'[14] The fact that the fossil record disagrees with this date by about fifteen million years did not bother Leslie in the least. After all, this information came straight from ancient Brahmin tables, and the Brahmins were not likely to be wrong. He goes on to say that 'Every legend, Greek, Roman, Egyptian, South American, Indian or Persian, of the gods coming to Earth can be traced back as a race memory of this one tremendous event.'[15] This was when 'true man' was created from 'animal-man', or as von Däniken would say, 'when man became intelligent.'[16] But von Däniken says that this occurred about forty thousand years ago, and not eighteen million years ago, as Leslie claimed. Just a minor discrepancy of about 17,060,000 years! But then, such disagreements are rather common among the various exponents of the ancient space-god theory.

Most U.F.O. contactee stories, however, are remarkably similar. Our earthling sees a flying saucer; the saucer lands; the occupant gets out and approaches the earthling and indicates concern over our world's problems in general or our atomic bombs in particular. The motives of spacemen are always spiritual or humanitarian in nature. Moreover, they look like human beings and either speak the dialect of the contactee or communicate by thought transference. As pointed out by Donald Menzel and Lyle Boyd in their book *The World of Flying Saucers*: 'Whether from Venus, Mars, Saturn, or the planets of other solar systems [the space visitors'] physical appearance, clothing, tastes in food, habits of thought, and ethical values usually seem indistinguishable from those of the citizens (whether American,

French, or Brazilian) who report the visitors.'[17] This assumption that extraterrestrials would be very similar to us is an example of what Carl Sagan calls our chauvinism. According to Sagan, 'The most likely circumstances is that extra-terrestrial beings will look nothing like any organisms or machines familiar to us.'[18]

Another example of a contactee case that exhibits both chauvinistic and religious characteristics is the episode claimed by Truman Bethurum, a construction worker and maintenance mechanic who, on the evening of 27 July 1952, happened to encounter a crew and lady captain of a spaceship from the planet 'Clarion'.

This event occurred in the Nevada desert on an otherwise calm Sunday evening, as a flying saucer crew of eight or ten little men caught Bethurum snoozing in the cab of his truck. A description of the spacemen is found in the Redondo Beach, California, *Daily Breeze* for 31 December 1953: 'the short men were "Latin types", that is, with complexions "something like Italians". All were neatly dressed in uniforms similar to those "worn by Greyhound bus drivers".'[19] The group took Bethurum by the hand and led him to their flying saucer. There he met the ravishing lady captain, named Aura Rhanes. She was seated at a desk in her cabin, and was described as having short black hair 'brushed into an upward curl at the ends' and wearing a 'black and red beret, tilted on the side of her head'.[20] Mrs Rhanes (who was said to have two grandchildren back on the planet Clarion) explained to Bethurum that the space travelers had come to earth because of our atomic explosions, which signaled to them our need for some cosmic guidance.[21] She also told him that on Clarion there were no such things as prisons, lawyers, guards at banks, and child delinquency. Nor was there any use of liquor or tobacco. The Clarionites were said to be very religious; they 'worship the "Supreme Entity, that sees all, knows all, and controls all".'[22] Bethurum later tried to establish a group dedicated to world peace.

Another contactee who formed a group for peace was

Dan Fry. Fry claimed an even earlier contact experience than either Adamski or Bethurum. On the fourth of July, 1950, so the story goes, Fry took a little stroll in the New Mexico desert near the White Sands Proving Ground, where he was employed at the time. He spotted a mysterious light in the sky, which came closer to him and assumed the shape of a giant silvery egg about thirty feet across at its greatest dimension. After the object had landed, Dan approached it and reached out to touch it. He was startled to hear a voice that seemed to be coming out of the air beside him, which said, 'Better not touch the hull, pal, it's still hot.'[23] Then, after a little introductory chat with the invisible spaceman (whose name was Alan), Fry was taken for a quick jaunt in the spacecraft to New York and back, a trip that lasted about thirty minutes.

This contactee case fits more closely than the others with the central theme of Erich von Däniken, since the saucer people who contacted Fry were supposedly the descendants of a past super-civilization on earth which was annihilated in an atomic war more than thirty thousand years ago. According to Alan, the saucerians' ancestors were originally from the legendary Lemuria, which was in scientific competition with the ancient civilization of Atlantis. These two nations eventually destroyed each other, except for the few survivors who were able to escape in four aerial craft capable of space travel. One ship was apparently lost along the way, but three landed on the planet Mars, where the survivors established a new society. Later they became independent of planets altogether and began living in huge self-sustaining ships that floated through space in whatever direction the people on them chose.

Other contactees that became the center of cults were George Van Tassell, the chief exponent of Outer Space Communications (through telepathy, of course) and master of ceremonies of the Giant Rock Space Convention;[24] Gabriel Green, head of Amalgamated Flying Saucer Clubs of America;[25] Howard Menger, who not only was contacted by extraterrestrials, but *married* one;[26] Orfeo Angelucci, a preacher of the gospel as revealed to him by the saucerians;[27] and the 'Reverend' George King, founder of the Aetherius Society.[28] What has been written about the latter organization could serve equally well as a commentary on the current ancient-astronaut cult:

> There can be little doubt that the cult developed in part as a response to the general uncertainty about outer space, the reported sightings of flying saucers and the increasing interest in the space research programmes of the major powers. Neither the teachings of the Churches nor the wisdom of science could give authoritative answers to the new range of questions which people were asking about space. For those unprepared to accept the reservations of cautious scientists, there may well be attractive qualities in a cult which claims to have positive answers to resolve their doubts. The Society offers this certain knowledge and, indeed, a direct means of contact with space people themselves. The Society's solution satisfies those who have come to the movement from leanings towards mysticism, those who have approached it with an interest simply in flying saucers, which are now given a positive role in the salvation of mankind, and those who are seeking a new interpretation of Christianity. The belief-system of the Aetherius Society has been successfully developed into a consistent and logically related pattern which provides a satisfying reinterpretation of existence for its members, who at the same time gain the status of the potential elect in the New Age of which they are the earthly handmaidens.[29]

No discussion on the religious-psychological aspects of flying saucer cults would be complete without mention of Carl Jung, the distinguished psychiatrist. In *Flying Saucers: A Modern Myth of Things Seen in the Skies*, he wrote: 'If these things [U.F.O.s] are real – and by all human standards it hardly seems possible to doubt this any longer – then we are left with only two hypotheses: that of their *weightlessness* on the one hand and of their *psychic nature* on the other.'[30] What occurred to Dr Jung was that thoughts and dreams are also weightless, and this he considered to be a clue to the psychic nature of U.F.O.s, with the suggestion that they are perhaps purely mental and have no existence outside the mind of the beholder. He regarded the U.F.O. phenomenon as a visionary rumor and as a psychological projection of man's hopes and fears in an uncertain world. This projection, in the form of circular shapes seen in the sky, represented to Jung man's perennial concept of God (or gods).

The following paragraphs set forth Jung's view of U.F.O.s:

> . . . one thing is certain: they have become a *living myth*. We have here a golden opportunity to see how a legend is formed, and how in a difficult and dark time for humanity a miraculous tale grows up of an attempted intervention by extra-terrestrial 'heavenly' powers – and this at the very time when human fantasy is seriously considering the possibility of space travel and of visiting or even invading other planets.[31]

> Anyone with the requisite historical and psychological knowledge knows that circular symbols have played an important role in every age; in our own sphere of culture, for instance, they were not only soul symbols but 'God-images'. There is an old saying that 'God is a circle whose centre is everywhere and the circumference nowhere'. God in his omniscience, omnipotence, and omnipresence is a totality symbol *par excellence*, something round, complete, and perfect. Epiphanies of this sort are, in the tradition, often associated with fire and light. On the antique level, therefore, the U.F.O.s could easily be conceived as 'gods'.[32]

Although the above quotations do not explain to my satisfaction the general phenomenon of U.F.O.s, they do, I believe, have much to say about the ancient astronaut theory.

The fact that cultists have seized upon flying saucers as a medium for religious expression should not detract from the serious aspects of U.F.O. phenomena and the studies conducted in recent years by reputable scientists, particularly the late James E. McDonald, atmospheric physicist of the University of Arizona, and J. Allen Hynek, astronomer at Northwestern University. Since 1947, there have been over twenty thousand reports of so-called unidentified flying objects. Many of these reports came from people of unquestionable integrity whose professional qualifications should not be taken lightly. What they have observed is open to interpretation and scientific debate, and should not be confused with the claims of contactees or other spiritualist cultists. But while keeping an open mind on the subject of U.F.O.s, a certain degree of skepticism should be maintained. The words of Arthur C. Clarke, writing in *The Promise of Space*, will illustrate the U.F.O. problem.

> ... about U.F.O.s, or flying saucers; whether their explanation is psychological or physical, they constitute one of the most remarkable phenomena of modern times. Unfortunately, it has become extraordinarily difficult to arrive at the truth in this matter; seldom has any subject been so invested with fraud, hysteria, credulity, religious mania, incompetence, and most of the other unflattering human characteristics. . . . There would be many fewer U.F.O.s around today if reason, or even elementary common sense, were in better supply.[33]

Close-up photo of the stone carving of the Palenque "astronaut".
His seat is the royal badge of rulership, atop the "Earth Monster".
No space-suit here; Pacal is wearing a breechcloth, jade belt,
anklets, and bracelets, and a jade necklace that looks like a cross
between a turtle and a scorpion. *From the film Chariots of the
Gods? By permission of Sun Classic Pictures, Inc.*

Above: Jabbaren, the "great Martian god". *Photo G. Franceschi, exclusivité Editions Arthaud. From A La Decouverte des Fresques du Tassili by H. Lhote, 1973, B. Arthaud, editeur, Grenoble, France*

Left: The open sarcophagus with the remains of Pacal, still "wearing" his jade ornaments. *From The Civilization of the Ancient Maya by Alberto Ruz Lhuillier, copyright 1970. By permission of the Instituto Nacional de Antropologia e Historia, Córdoba, Mexico*

Above: The rustproof iron pillar near Delhi, India. *Information Service of India, New York*

Right: Elephantine Island, which looks more like a spaceship than an elephant. *From the Map Collection of the American Geographical Society, New York*

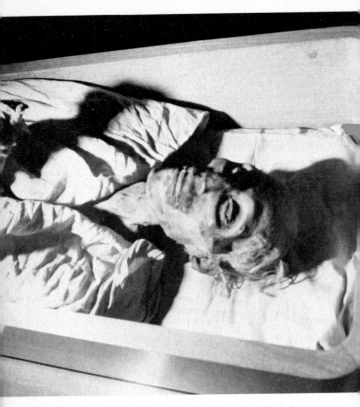

Above: Egyptian
mummy at the Cairo
Museum. *From the
film The Outer Space
Connection. By
permission of Sun
Classic Pictures, Inc.*

Right: Section of a
map drawn by Percival
Lowell, dated 1895,
showing canal network
in the Meridiani Sinus
region of Mars.

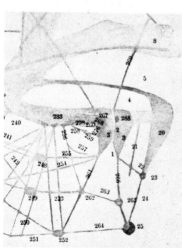

The Meridiani Sinus region of Mars photographed by *Mariner 9* and processed by computer contrast-enhancement technique. Craters and dark areas stand out clearly, but the photograph does not show the long, straight "canals" recorded by the early observers. *Official NASA photo*

Close-up view of the
Martian moon Phobos,
showing it to be a
potato-shaped ''rock''
covered with craters.
Computer-processed
photo taken in 1971 by
*Mariner 9. Official
NASA photo*

15

The New Mythology

Myths have served man well in helping him adapt to a sometimes confusing and mystifying world. Today, an accelerating technology threatens our mental equilibrium. We are verging on 'future shock', Alvin Toffler's term for 'the shattering stress and disorientation that we induce in individuals by subjecting them to too much change in too short a time'.[1] At the same time, in our first venture into space, we are infatuated with our own technology and look to it as a solution to our problems.

Man's inability to rise to a high moral plane, even in times of dire need, is all too evident in the present world situation with its threat of atomic war, depletion of natural resources, and widespread hunger. Just as in the days of the contactees and the 'Space Brothers', we are facing bad times and fears of the future – fears of an ever-advancing technology that seems to be running out of control.

What could be more appealing than the modern Space Brothers – the ancient astronauts of von Däniken, who are godlike in their technical knowledge (which is so threatening but means so much to us) and in their wisdom (so we assume), and who could direct us in the use of advanced knowledge for the ultimate good of mankind? Since the gods may be our salvation, we *want* to believe in them, whether we realize it or not. By identifying with these gods, we both comfort our fears and flatter our egos.

The whole von Däniken affair, it would seem, represents a modern mythology couched in space-technology symbols. Here are reconciled elements of ancient and modern mythology and a literal truth of the Bible. Those who want to accept the literal truth of the Bible (or other sacred texts) but would like to dispense with its moral teachings, at least in actual practice, can have a natural basis for their beliefs instead of the traditional supernatural one. And those who miss the sense of awe and mystery their abandoned religions provided can find it again in the cult of the ancient astronauts.

Elements of the current nostalgia craze also seem to be present. We can look back upon a 'golden age' of the ancient past when there were leaders and heroes worthy of respect. And with our chances of long-term survival now a giant question mark, we hope the 'gods' will return.

There is also the perennial problem of boredom. Throughout history, man has sought new ways of alleviating his boredom, from casual amusements and distractions to arduous journeys and colossal construction projects. This problem is with us today as strongly as ever. Certainly beings from other worlds would be interesting. Once communication was established, we could ply them with endless questions about themselves, their customs, and their technology. And who knows, they might even let us ride in one of their spaceships!

It is interesting to see the ancient symbolism of rebirth emerging in a modern-day cult based on space travel. Free from earth's gravity, we may be spiritually regenerated in space and return with new insights. Perhaps we hope to be as the star-child of *2001: A Space Odyssey*, whose rebirth promised nothing less than salvation.

A characteristic of many ancient myths is the twin god-head: the benefactor for Good and the scapegoat for Evil. In the New Mythlogoy, the astronaut-gods are primarily benefactors for good. However, they also may personify evil. A recent study undertaken by the Center for Policy Research under the direction of Dr Clyde Z. Nunn showed that from 1964 to 1973, belief in the existence of the devil increased from 37 percent to 48 percent. A news article entitled 'Demonic Believers Increase' says that Dr Nunn 'attributes the growing popular belief in the devil to a mood of "uncertainty and stress, when things seem to be falling apart and resources seem limited for coping with it". Nunn suggested that in a fearful world people tend to look for "scapegoats" such as the devil.'[2] Perhaps, then, it is not just coincidence that books should be published about ancient astronauts bearing such titles as *Gods, Demons, and Space Chariots* and *Gods and Devils from Outer Space*.[3] In fact, von Däniken is quoted by the *National Enquirer* as stating that he believes Satan was indeed an astronaut.[4]

And so it is not difficult to see how such a myth as von Däniken's could grow up in the modern world. It fulfills remarkably well the functions of a living mythology as formulated by Joseph Campbell:

> The first is ... the mystical function: to waken and maintain in the individual a sense of awe and gratitude in relation to the mystery dimensions of the universe, not so that he lives in fear of it, but so that he recognizes that he participates in it, since the mystery of being is the mystery of his own deep being as well. ...
>
> The second function of a living mythology is to offer an image of the universe that will be in accord with the knowledge of the time, the sciences and the fields of action of the folk to whom the mythology is addressed. ...
>
> The third function ... is to validate, support, and imprint the norms of a given, specific moral order, that, namely, of the society in which the individual is to live. And the fourth is to guide him, stage by stage, in health, strength, and harmony of spirit, through the whole foreseeable course of a useful life.[5]

The ancient astronaut theory does seem to represent to many people a solution to the uncertainties that now plague the world. If the space-gods are bestowers of kindness, we need not solve our own problems; our benefactors will take care of us when they return. Such a belief can only serve to divert our attention from human concerns and human responsibility. If our planet is to survive, if social injustices are ever to be rectified, and if we are ever to have an ethical society, we must practice all forms of honesty. This includes distinguishing carefully between science and pseudoscience. Wild speculations in the guise of science and a collection of half-truths will only retard our progress.

Appendix

U.F.O.s and the Bible: A Review of the Literature*
by Dr Robert S. Ellwood, Jr., Professor of Religion
University of Southern California

For nearly twenty-five years now, books of all sorts have appeared
on the U.F.O. problem. A certain category of them has attempted
to isolate U.F.O.-type objects and the works of spacemen in man's
ancient religions, mythologies, and symbols. As might be expected
since most of the books have been written in the West, more emphasis
in this connection has been placed on the Christian Bible than any
other source. In order to get some idea of the manner of books which
these studies have produced, I have examined a number of them:
Adrian V. Clark, *Cosmic Mysteries of the Universe* (West Nyack,
N.Y., 1968); Erich von Däniken, *Chariots of the Gods?* (New York,
1970) and *Gods from Outer Space* (New York, 1968); John W. Dean,
Flying Saucers and the Scriptures (New York, 1964); Barry H. Down-
ing, *The Bible and Flying Saucers* (New York, 1968); R. L. Dione, *God
Drives a Flying Saucer* (New York, 1969); Ulysee Douglas, *The
Phenomena of Flying Saucers and Spatial People* (New York, 1969);
W. R. Drake, *Gods or Spacemen?* (Amherst, Wisconsin, 1964) and
Spacemen in the Ancient East (London, n.d.); M. K. Jessup, *U.F.O.
and the Bible* (New York, 1956); R. Cedric Leonard, *Flying Saucers,*

* © *Aerial Phenomena Research Organization (A.P.R.O.) Bulletin* (September–
October 1971). Reprinted with permission.

Ancient Writings and the Bible (New York, 1969); Desmond Leslie and George Adamski, *Flying Saucers Have Landed* (New York, 1953); Eric Norman, *Gods, Demons, and U.F.O.s* (New York, 1970); Paul Thomas, *Flying Saucers Through the Ages* (London, 1965); Brinsley Le Poer Trench, *The Sky People* (London, 1960).

I cannot claim to have read all of these works, despite their intriguing titles. Frankly, the general level of scholarship is so low, and of pretentious but turgid writing so high, I do not see how any balanced person with equal access to, say, P. G. Wodehouse could do so. The quality of most of these books does differ within a low range, and the patient reader is very occasionally rewarded in the best with a mildly, thought-provoking insight. But my first reaction after reading as much as I could take of the material was to feel I must decline the piece on them Richard Greenwell (former editor of the A.P.R.O. Bulletin) confidently asked me to do. My general impression was of a hopeless mass of woolly theories and garbled facts by authors obviously innocent of most of what is known of the language and cultural background of the ancient books, and of the canons of rational thinking. Although quotations from sources arcane to the general public, such as the *Mahabharata* and the *Book of Enoch*, may appear at first glance impressive, a little comparison indicates that our writers mostly borrow from each other. Moreover, the translations and secondary souces they employ tend to be very dated and not the best. Desmond Leslie, a wide-ranging researcher of 'occultist' bent, seems to have accumulated most of the stock citations which later authors have picked up. Leslie, however, weakens the confidence one might have in some of his interesting cases by setting it alongside dilations on pseudo-sources of modern origin.

I felt at first that I could take one or two courses in response to this material. I could exhaustively go through all the thousands of pages before me, discussing all the apparent errors of faulty research, interpretation, and logic. Or, I could ignore the books. I had not the time nor motivation for the former Augean task, nor in every case the credentials. I was inclined to set the paper aside. The problem is that weak scholarship is really more difficult to refute than good, and the job more thankless, for poor scholars are usually harder to convince in their follies. Every teacher knows it takes more work to correct a bad paper than a good one. Our writers, like sloppy students, confuse names (like calling the last Book of the Bible 'Revelations' rather than 'Revelation'), use inadequate documentation, show no critical control of sources, make no linguistic analysis of terms, show no background sophistication in understanding the role of symbols like wheel and sun in a Bible allusion or a culture under discussion. The critic would have not only to do all this for them, but also explain what satisfactory methodology is.

I am not about to do this. Therefore, if any reader wants to know why I hold the books are mostly nonsense on the historical and factual level, his curiosity will have to remain unsatisfied. If he feels I am retreating behind academic snobbery, sorry about that! If anyone wants to believe that every cloud in the Bible is a 'code' for a U.F.O., or that because Jesus said, 'I am the bright and morning star', he must have been a Master come from Venus, I will not argue. For examples of demolishing analysis applied to a few stock cases allegedly from ancient myth and history used by writers of the sort under discussion, see the Condon Report,* pp. 493–501. Of course, the fact that most people in any field have better things to do than refute at length every pretentious but careless privately printed presentation that comes along is what leads those who write such things to claim there is a 'conspiracy of silence' against them by dogmatic 'orthodox' science or scholarship.

Next, however, I considered another tack I could take in trying to understand these books. I could endeavor not to look at the details of the arguments, but to strive to understand the passions, and the worldview, of people for whom they are lively and important. I was convinced and still am, that the Bible and the U.F.O. problem are both important, but that the former has no more to do with the latter than it does with the scientific study of stellar atmospheres. But one can ask the significant question: Why is it important to some people to see U.F.O.s in the Bible and in ancient myths and symbols around the world? In trying to answer this query, I looked at the books in a new light: for their dominant unspoken assumptions and for the furniture of their authors' cosmos. This is what I found:

1. Very important to the writers is the matter of the confrontation of sciences and religion. For them the terms boil down to this: 'science' means the appalling vastness of the modern universe, the prestige of technology, and the discrediting of pre-scientific religious concepts; 'religion' means the authority of the Bible and a nagging idea that somehow the 'ancients' must have known something too. They resolve the confrontation not in the usual way, that science gives us facts and religion gives us humanistically meaningful 'symbols' and 'values', but in another way. The Bible is literally true, the old

* E. U. Condon, *Scientific Study of Unidentified Flying Objects* (New York: Bantam Books, 1969).

myths tell things that really happened, but its meaning could not have been comprehended until the technological age, with its awareness of the universe of modern astronomy and of space-flight. The angels and saviours of old were really extra-terrestrial astronauts!

2. Hence, in a modern world which too often seems given over to Blake's deadly 'number, weight, and measure', if not worse horrors, these writers find in the U.F.O.s 'technological angels', in Jung's term: envoys of cosmic life and wonder and marvel and help on a scale equal to the great religious visions of the past – which is proved by the fact that they are what really lay behind the religions too! They are people desperate in quest of that noblest and rarest of human boons, an experience of wonder, and when the U.F.O.s bestow it, they cannot but believe the Ultimate must lie encapsuled in them. Technological and scientific awe becomes religious awe, the U.F.O. becomes the numinous; and then by a natural conflation past religion becomes the U.F.O.

The process is splendidly illustrated in Barry Downing's book. I hasten to say that, while I do not find it really convincing, this book is head and shoulders above the others named. The writer has a good modern theological education, and a deep and intelligent concern over the plight of religion in today's world. He reviews with understanding the problem modern scientifically educated man has in believing religious notions, such as angelic visitations, miracles, and the ascension of Jesus, described in the Bible with the perspective of a pre-scientific worldview. He talks of how theologians like Bultmann, Bishops Robinson and Pike, and the 'Death of God' school have sincerely tried to overcome the gap by setting aside all that is incredible today and leaving only the moral and existential 'core' of religion. Many, including myself, can sympathize with Downing's conundrum: he is not prepared to reject or compartmentalize out science in the manner of the Fundamentalists, but he is equally distressed at the drab faith left by the 'demythologizers', whose religion seems to be decapitated of all sense of transcendence and wonder. His solution is to bring the U.F.O. to the rescue. The major events of the Bible, from the Exodus to the Ascension, really happened, but were accomplished by vastly superior Guardians operating with U.F.O.s. Downing is refreshingly modest in his argument; he only 'about 80 percent' believes that the parting of the Red Sea waters was accomplished by U.F.O.

3. Finally, in this same vein, the U.F.O.-Bible-myth alignment becomes for our writers a key to understanding personal experience,

whether he is an initiated 'contactee' or just a troubled religious seeker. The problem with being human is that sometimes we feel an inner expansive joy, godlike and more piercing than all grief, and sometimes we feel like klutzes beyond hope, stupid, lost, hurting, the eternal fire banked by pounds of clay. Interpreting the existence of these two 'persons' within the same body and soul has been the root problem of religious teaching. In some way, metaphysical or biological of both, mankind must have two origins, earth and starry heaven.

The U.F.O. theologies are mostly efforts to create new myths, in the light of the U.F.O. experience, to explain this human condition. Many are very literal-minded statements that we have in us the blood of a cosmic race: Adam was born of the animal and the U.F.O. occupant. Some make it a double election; some humans are really cosmic, others earthly. Our space brothers, Guardians and Shepherds of their kin toiling here below, have kept in touch and have tried to prepare us for final realization of our splendid origin and destiny: Elijah's chariot, Ezekiel's wheels, Jesus' ascension. Now they are coming back. The Biblical drama of God's reaching to man through crisis and the moments of ecstasy becomes read in light of what is for certain people today the central symbol of ultimate transcendence: the U.F.O. with its mysterious origin and its marvelous freedom in the Universe.

These books may be pitiful stumbling efforts in the morasses of technical and historical scholarship, and rather too much *tours de force* for pet ideas. But as religion they are worthy of respect as picture-language wrestling with the deep matters all persons face – or evade – in the stillness of the heart. On this level their scientific and historical failings may not matter so much. In what pertains to the ultimate beyond the circles of science and history, all language is picture-language only shadowing what is beyond words. It is, in the old Zen phrase, the finger pointing at the moon.

Source Notes

1. THE VON DÄNIKEN PHENOMENON

1. *Beyond Reality*, April 1974, p. 58.
2. *Der Spiegel* No. 12/1969 (17 March 1969), p. 184; No. 12/1973 (19 March 1973), p. 145.
3. Louis Pauwels and Jacques Bergier, *The Morning of the Magicians*, trans. Rollo Myers (New York: Stein and Day, 1964; paperback ed. Avon, 1968; London: Anthony Gibbs & Phillips, 1963). Originally published as *Le Matin des Magiciens* (Paris: Editions Gallimard, 1960).
4. Robert Charroux, *One Hundred Thousand Years of Man's Unknown History*, trans. Lowell Bair (New York: Berkley, Medallion Books, 1971). Published in Paris by Robert Laffont, 1963.
5. *Der Spiegel* No. 12/1969, p. 185.
6. Timothy Ferris, interview with Erich von Däniken, *Playboy*, vol. 21, no. 8 (August 1974), p. 51.
7. Erich von Däniken, *Gods from Outer Space*, trans. Michael Heron (New York: Bantham Books, 1972), p. x. Published in hard cover by G. P. Putnam's Sons, New York, 1971; Souvenir Press, London, 1970.
8. Ibid., p. vii.
9. 'Auch ein Erfolgsautor muss sich ans Gesetz halten,' *Tages-Anzeiger*, 4 February 1971.

2. THE THEORY AND THE 'PROOF'

1. *Playboy*, p. 64.
2. Erich von Däniken, *Chariots of the Gods?*, trans. Michael Heron (New York: Bantam Books, 1971), p. 13. Published in hard cover by G. P. Putnam's Sons, New York, 1970; Souvenir Press, London, 1969.
3. Ibid., p. viii.
4. Bertrand Russell, *An Outline of Philosophy* (New York: World, Meridian Books, 1960), p. 7. Published in hard cover by W. W. Norton, New York, 1927, under the title *Philosophy*; George Allen & Unwin, London, 1927.
5. *Chariots of the Gods?*, pp. 66–67.
6. Ibid., pp. 51–52.
7. Ibid, p. 52.
8. Erich von Däniken, *The Gold of the Gods*, trans. Michael Heron (New York: Bantam Books, 1974), pp. 212–15. Published in hard cover by G. P. Putnam's Sons, New York, 1973; Souvenir Press, London, 1973.
9. Ibid., p. 36.
10. *Chariots of the Gods?*, p. 98.
11. Ibid., p. 25.
12. Ibid., p. 31.
13. Ibid., p. 12.
14. Ibid., pp. 86–87.
15. Ibid., p. 32.
16. Ibid., p. 17.
17. Ibid., pp. 40–41.
18. Ibid., p. 30.
19. Ibid., p. 35.
20. *Playboy*, p. 51.

3. ANCIENT ASTRONAUTS AND THE BIBLE

1. M. K. Jessup, *U.F.O. and the Bible* (New York: Citadel Press, 1956), p. 98.
2. Brinsley Le Poer Trench, *The Sky People* (London: Neville Spearman, 1960).
3. Arthur Gorlick, 'History or Good Fiction?' *Arizona Daily Star*, 16 September 1973 (original source: *Chicago Daily News*, 1973).

4. *Chariots of the Gods?*, p. 34.
5. *The Oxford Annotated Bible with the Apocrypha*, Revised Standard Version, ed. Herbert G. May and Bruce M. Metzger (New York: Oxford University Press, 1965), p. 2.
6. *The Interpreter's Bible* (Nashville, Tenn.: Abingdon Press, 1952), vol. 1, p. 483.
7. Ibid., p. 482.
8. *Chariots of the Gods?*, p. 35.
9. *The Oxford Annotated Bible*, p. 8.
10. Ibid.
11. *The Interpreter's Bible*, vol. 1, p. 533.
12. *Chariots of the Gods?*, pp. 36–37.
13. Werner Keller, *The Bible as History*, trans. William Neil (New York: William Morrow, 1956), p. 77. Paperback ed. Bantam Books, 1974.
14. Ibid., p. 81.
15. Robert T. Boyd, *Tells, Tombs and Treasure* (New York: Baker Book House, 1969), p. 86. (Reprinted by Bonanza Books.)
16. *Chariots of the Gods?*, p. 37.
17. F. N. Peloubet and Alice D. Adams, *Peloubet's Bible Dictionary* (New York: Holt, Rinehart and Winston, 1947), p. 116.
18. C. P. S. Menon, *Early Astronomy and Cosmology* (London: George Allen & Unwin, 1932), p. 141.
19. *Chariots of the Gods?*, p. 39.
20. Josef F. Blumrich, *The Spaceships of Ezekiel* (New York: Bantam Books, 1974), p. 2.
21. Ibid., p. 3.
22. Ibid., p. 57.
23. Ibid., p. 58.
24. *The Gold of the Gods*, p. 221.
25. Donald H. Menzel, 'U.F.O.'s – The Modern Myth', *U.F.O.'s – A Scientific Debate*, ed. by Carl Sagan and Thornton Page (Ithaca, N.Y.: Cornell University Press, 1972), pp. 177–78. Paperback ed. W. W. Norton, 1974.
26. Ibid., p. 178.
27. Barry H. Downing, *The Bible and Flying Saucers* (Philadelphia and New York: J. B. Lippincott, 1968). Paperback ed. Avon, 1970.
28. Trench, p. 80.
29. Downing, p. 113.

30. Trench, p. 81.
31. Downing, p. 81.

4. A GENETIC MIRACLE

1. *Gods from Outer Space*, p. 13.
2. Ibid., p. 15.
3. Ibid., p. 26.
4. Ibid., p. 146.
5. *Chariots of the Gods?*, p. 65.

5. THE PIRI RE'IS MAP

1. *Playboy*, p. 64.
2. Erich von Däniken, *In Search of Ancient Gods*, trans. Michael Heron (New York: Bantam Books, 1975), p. 136. Published in hard cover by G. P. Putnam's Sons, New York, 1974; Souvenir Press, London, 1973).
3. *Piri Re'is Haritasi, Türk Tarihi Arastirma Kurumu Yayinlarindan: No. 1* (Istanbul: Devlet Basimevi, 1935), p. 12.
4. Charles H. Hapgood, *Maps of the Ancient Sea Kings* (Philadelphia and New York: Chilton Books, 1966).
5. *Chariots of the Gods?*, pp. 14–16.
6. Hapgood, pp. 37–38.
7. Ibid., p. 77.
8. Ibid., p. 68.
9. Ibid., Preface.
10. Louis Pauwels and Jacques Bergier, *The Morning of the Magicians* (New York: Stein & Day, 1960), p. 120.
11. Donald E. Keyhoe, *Flying Saucers: Top Secret* (New York: G. P. Putnam's Sons, 1960), p. 212.
12. Pauwels and Bergier, p. 120.
13. Charroux, p. 16.

6. THE NAZCA PLAIN

1. George Hunt Williamson, *Road in the Sky* (London: Neville Spearman, 1959), pp. 65 ff.
2. *Chariots of the Gods?*, p. 17.
3. Paul Kosok, with the collaboration of Maria Reiche, 'The Mysterious Markings of Nazca', *Natural History*, May 1947, p. 202. Also, for other detailed accounts of the views of Pau

Kosok and Maria Reiche, see their article entitled 'Ancient Drawings on the Desert of Peru', *Archaeology*, December 1949; Paul Kosok's book *Life, Land and Water in Ancient Peru* (New York: Long Island University Press, 1965), chap. 6, 'The Largest Astronomy Book in the World: New Aspects of Ancient Nazca'; and Maria Reiche's book *Mystery on the Desert* (privately published by Maria Reiche, 7 Stuttgart-Vaihingen, Lutzweg 9, Germany, 1968).

4. Gerald S. Hawkins, *Beyond Stonehenge* (New York: Harper & Row, 1973), p. 115.
5. *Chariots of the Gods?*, p. 10.
6. In Loren McIntyre, 'Mystery of the Ancient Nazca Lines', *National Geographic*, May 1975, p. 718.
7. In Jim Woodman, 'New Mysteries in Ancient Peru', *Braniff Place*, vol. 4, no. 5 (1975), p. 33.
8. Louis Pauwels and Jacques Bergier, *The Morning of the Magicians*, trans. Rollo Myers (New York: Avon Books, 1968), p. 176.
9. *Time*, 15 December 1975, p. 50.

7. EASTER ISLAND

1. *Gods from Outer Space*, p. 116.
2. Ibid.
3. Ibid.
4. Thor Heyerdahl, *Aku-Aku* (Chicago: Rand McNally, 1958), pp. 136–37. Paperback ed. Pocket Books, 1960.
5. *Gods from Outer Space*, p. 119.
6. Ibid., p. 120.
7. Heyerdahl, p. 91.
8. *Chariots of the Gods?*, p. 90.
9. Ibid., p. 91.
10. *Gods from Outer Space*, p. 116.
11. William Mulloy, 'A Speculative Reconstruction of Techniques of Carving, Transporting, and Erecting Easter Island Statues', *Archaeology & Physical Anthropology in Oceania*, vol. 5, no. 1 (April 1970), p. 2.
12. *Chariots of the Gods?*, p. 91.
13. Ibid., p. 92.
14. *Gods from Outer Space*, p. 116.
15. Mulloy, p. 9.

16. Ibid., pp. 9–10.
17. Ibid., p. 8.

8. THE EGYPTIAN PYRAMIDS

1. *Chariots of the Gods?*, p. 74.
2. Ibid.
3. Kurt Mendelssohn, *The Riddle of the Pyramids* (New York: Praeger, 1974), p. 18. (See also Mendelssohn's earlier article, 'A Scientist Looks at the Pyramids', *American Scientists*, March–April 1971, p. 218.)
4. Ibid.
5. *Chariots of the Gods?*, p. 77.
6. See Martin Gardner's 'Mathematical Games', *Scientific American*, June 1974, p. 117. See also 'The Great Pyramid, the Golden Section and Pi', an essay by Willy Ley, in his book *Another Look at Atlantis* (Garden City, N.Y.: Doubleday, 1969). (Reprinted by Bell, New York, n.d.), pp. 27 ff.
7. *Chariots of the Gods?*, pp. 75, 78.
8. George Steindorff and Keith C. Seele, *When Egypt Ruled the East* (Chicago and London: University of Chicago Press, 1942, 1957), p. 21.
9. *Chariots of the Gods?*, p. 77.

9. THE PALENQUE ASTRONAUT

1. *Gods from Outer Space*, p. 113.
2. *Chariots of the Gods?*, pp. 100–1.
3. Ibid., p. 100.
4. Ibid., p. 93.
5. Norman Hammond, 'The Maya Jade Trade: Source Locations and Analyses and Artifact Attributions', a paper read at the annual meeting of the Society for American Archaeology in May 1974, Dallas, Texas.
6. Alberto Ruz Lhuillier, *The Civilization of the Ancient Maya* (Córdoba, Mexico: Instituto Nacional de Antropologia e Historia, 1970), pp. 119–20.
7. Peter Mathews and Linda Schele, 'Lords of Palenque – The Glyphic Evidence', *Primera Mesa Redonda de Palenque: A Conference on the Art, Iconography, and Dynastic History of Palenque*, Part 1, Merle Greene Robertson, ed. (Pebble Beach,

Calif.: Robert Louis Stevenson School, 1974), pp. 63 ff.

8. Ibid., Parts *I* and *II*.
9. Ruz Lhuillier, p. 120.
10. Ibid., p. 118.
11. Ibid., p. 120.
12. Merle Greene Robertson, 'The Quadripartite Badge – A Badge of Rulership', *Primera Mesa Redonda de Palenque*, Part I, p. 79.
13. Ibid., pp. 81–82.

10. CAVES FILLED WITH GOLD

1. *The Gold of the Gods*, p. 21.
2. Ibid., p. 3.
3. Ibid., p. 1.
4. *Der Spiegel*, No. 12/1973 (19 March 1973), pp. 156, 158–59. Trans. Joseph L. Scott.
5. *Der Spiegel*, No. 36/1972 (28 August 1972), p. 118.
6. *Playboy*, p. 58.
7. *Der Spiegel*, No. 36/1972, p. 120.
8. John Keasler, 'Von Däniken's "Golden Gods": Great Find or Great Fraud?' *Miami News*, 17 October 1973.
9. Ibid.

11. OTHER STRANGE 'EVIDENCE'

1. *Chariots of the Gods?*, p. 18.
2. Ibid., pp. 21–22.
3. Ibid., pp. 18–19.
4. Ibid., pp. 27–28.
5. Ibid., p. 93.
6. As advertised in the September 1974 issue of *National Geographic*.
7. *Chariots of the Gods?*, p. 31.
8. Jean-Dominique Lajoux, *The Rock Paintings of Tassili*, trans. G. D. Liversage (Cleveland and New York: World Publishing, 1963), pp. 31–32, 34, 38–73.
9. Henri Lhote, *The Search for the Tassili Frescoes*, trans. A. Broderick (New York: E. P. Dutton, 1959), pp. 104–5.
10. Ibid., pp. 78–79.
11. *Gods from Outer Space*, p. 67.
12. Ibid., p. 68.
13. *National Enquirer*, 24 December 1974, p. 4.

14. Lee Emerson, 'Petroglyphs of Ancient Man', *The Indian Historian*, vol. 4, no. 1 (1971), pp. 5–8.
15. *Chariots of the Gods?*, p. 73.
16. A. L. Basham, *The Wonder That Was India* (New York: Grove Press, 1954), p. 220.
17. *Playboy*, p. 64.
18. *Chariots of the Gods?*, p. 63.
19. Emil Ludwig, *The Nile: The Life-Story of a River*, trans. Mary H. Lindsay (New York: Viking Press, 1937), p. 348.
20. *A Lexicon Abridged from Liddell & Scott's Greek-English Lexicon* (London: Oxford University Press, 1963), p. 215.

12. EXTRATERRESTRIAL SCIENCE?

1. Interview with Stanley Kubrick in *Playboy* (September 1968), reprinted in *The Making of Kubrick's 2001*, ed. Jerome Agel (New York: Signet Books, 1968), pp. 330–32.
2. Aidan Cockburn, Robin A. Barraco, Theodore A. Reyman, and William H. Peck, 'Autopsy of an Egyptian Mummy', *Science*, 28 March 1975, pp. 1155 ff.
3. *Chariots of the Gods?*, p. 78.
4. Ibid., p. 40.
5. Ibid., p. 41.
6. Albert Al-Haik, 'The Rabbou'a Galvanic Cell', *Sumer*, vol. 20 (1964), pp. 103–4. See also W. Winton, 'Baghdad Batteries B.C.', *Sumer*, vol. 18 (1962), pp. 87–89.
7. *Chariots of the Gods?*, p. 11.
8. *Playboy*, p. 56.

13. THE MYSTERIOUS MOONS OF MARS

1. Patrick Moore, *A Guide to the Planets* (New York: W. W. Norton, 1954, 1960), p. 115.
2. From a reprint of a paper by Carl Sagan and Paul Fox, entitled 'The Canals of Mars: An Assessment After Mariner 9' and from Carl Sagan's *The Cosmic Connection* (New York: Doubleday/Anchor, 1973), p. 130.
3. Jonathan Swift, *Gulliver's Travels* (New York: Crown, Bonanza Books, 1947), p. 193. A modern facsimile edition of the original, which was first published in 1726.
4. I. S. Shklovskii and Carl Sagan, *Intelligent Life in the Universe*

(New York: Dell, Delta Books, 1968), p. 363. Published in hard cover by Holden-Day, San Francisco, 1966.

5. Immanuel Velikovsky, *Worlds in Collision* (New York: Macmillan, 1950), p. 280. Also published by Doubleday, 1950. Paperback ed. Dell, Delta Books, 1965.

6. Joseph F. Goodavage, *Astrology: The Space Age Science* (New York: Signet Books, 1967), p. 98. Published in hard cover by Parker, West Nyack, N.Y., 1966.

7. Gerald Heard, *The Riddle of the Flying Saucers – Is Another World Watching?* (London: Carroll & Nicholson, 1950), p. 127.

8. *Chariots of the Gods?*, p. 128.

9. Personal correspondence, August 13, 1974.

10. *Playboy*, p. 151.

11. *Chariots of the Gods?*, p. 128.

12. 'Three Spacecraft Study the Red Planet,' *Sky & Telescope*, January 1972, p. 16; J. B. Pollack et al., 'Mariner 9 Television Observations of Phobos and Deimos, 2', *Journal of Geophysical Research*, 10 July 1973, pp. 4313–26.

13. J. B. Pollack et al., 'Mariner 9 Television Observations of Phobos and Deimos', *Icarus*, October 1972, p. 406.

14. 'GODS' IN RECENT TIMES

1. From an article, 'Radio Listeners in Panic, Taking War Drama as Fact', *The New York Times*, 31 October 1938.

2. Martin Gardner, *Fads & Fallacies in the Name of Science* (New York: Dover, 1957), p. 67.

3. Kenneth Arnold and Ray Palmer, *The Coming of the Saucers* (privately published by the authors, copyright, 1952, by Ray Palmer, Amherst, Wisc), p. 11.

4. Kenneth Arnold, 'I *Did* See the Flying Disks', *Fate*, vol. 1, no. 1 (Spring 1948).

5. Donald Keyhoe, *The Flying Saucers Are Red* (New York: Fawcett, 1950).

6. Edward U. Condon, 'U.F.O.s: 1947–1968', *Scientific Study of Unidentified Flying Objects*, ed. Daniel S. Gillmor (New York: E. P. Dutton, 1969), p. 510. Paperback ed. Bantam Books, 1969.

7. Edward J. Ruppelt, *The Report on Unidentified Flying Objects* (Garden City, N.Y.: Doubleday, 1956), p. 65. Paperback ed. Ace Books, 1956.

8. Donald Keyhoe, *Flying Saucers from Outer Space* (New York: Henry Holt, 1953), pp. 225 ff.

9. Robert S. Ellwood, Jr., *Religious and Spiritual Groups in Modern America* (Englewood Cliffs, N.J.: Prentice-Hall, 1973), p. 131.

10. Desmond Leslie and George Adamski, *Flying Saucers Have Landed* (New York: British Book Centre, 1953), p. 185.

11. Ibid., p. 195.

12. Ibid., p. 199.

13. George Adamski, *Inside the Space Ships* (London: Abelard-Schuman, 1955). Paperback ed. (*Inside the Flying Saucers*) Warner Paperback Library, 1967.

14. Leslie and Adamski, pp. 164–65.

15. Ibid., p. 167.

16. *Gods from Outer Space*, p. 15.

17. Donald H. Menzel and Lyle G. Boyd, *The World of Flying Saucers* (Garden City, N.Y.: Doubleday, 1963), p. 200.

18. Carl Sagan, *The Cosmic Connection* (Garden City, N.Y.: Doubleday, Anchor Press, 1973), p. 41. Paperback ed. Dell, 1975.

19. Reprinted in *Valor – The Golden Times Weekly*, Noblesville, Ind., 6 February 1954.

20. Gavin Gibbons, *They Rode in Space Ships* (New York: Citadel Press, 1957), p. 120.

21. T. M. Wright, *The Intelligent Man's Guide to Flying Saucers* (New York: A. S. Barnes, 1968), p. 206.

22. From the *Daily Express*, reprinted in *Valor.*

23. Gibbons, p. 11.

24. Ellwood, pp. 141–43.

25. Ibid., pp. 145–49.

26. Howard Menger, *From Outer Space to You* (Clarksburg, W. Va.: Saucerian Books, 1959).

27. Carl G. Jung, *Flying Saucers: A Modern Myth of Things Seen in the Skies* (New York: Signet Books, 1969), pp. 119–27. Published in hard cover by Harcourt, Brace & World, New York, 1959.

28. J. A. Jackson, 'Man, Myth and Magic', *The Illustrated Encyclopedia of the Supernatural* (New York: Marshall Cavendish, 1970), vol. 8, pp. 1003–4.

29. Ibid., p. 1004.

30. Jung, p. 116.

31. Ibid., p. 27.

32. Ibid, p. 32.

33. Arthur C. Clarke, *The Promise of Space* (New York: Harper & Row, 1968), pp. 301, 302. Paperback ed. Pyramid Books, 1970.

15. THE NEW MYTHOLOGY

1. Alvin Toffler, *Future Shock* (New York: Bantam Books, 1971), p. 2. Published in hard cover by Random House, New York, 1970.
2. 'Demonic Believers Increase,' *Tucson Daily Citizen*, 4 April 1974. Original source: AP, New York.
3. Both written by Eric Norman (pen name for Warren Smith) and published by Lancer Books of New York in 1970 and 1973 respectively. Especially interesting are references to Bob Geyer, and his 'Church of Jesus the Saucerian'.
4. 'The Devil Was an Astronaut,' *National Enquirer*, 27 May 1975, p. 5.
5. Joseph Campbell, *Myths to Live By* (New York: Bantam Books 1973), pp. 221–22. Published in hard cover by Viking Press, New York, 1972.

Index

151

THE BERMUDA TRIANGLE MYSTERY—SOLVED

by Lawrence David Kusche

Seaquakes. Waterspouts. Time warps. Black holes in space. Freak seas. UFOs collecting earthlings and whisking them off to other galaxies. All these and more have been advanced as explanations of the puzzle of the Bermuda Triangle.

Lawrence David Kusche has assembled all the evidence available, disentangled fact from fiction and presented his account in such a way as to allow the reader to unravel the problems – and, like himself, solve the mystery.

NEW ENGLISH LIBRARY

NEL

21

YEARS

BESTSELLERS

T035 794	HOW GREEN WAS MY VALLEY	*Richard Llewellyn*	95p
T039 560	I BOUGHT A MOUNTAIN	*Thomas Firbank*	90p
T033 988	IN TEETH OF THE EVIDENCE	*Dorothy L. Sayers*	90p
T040 755	THE KING MUST DIE	*Macy Renault*	85p
T038 149	THE CARPETBAGGERS	*Harold Robbins*	£1.50
T040 917	TO SIR WITH LOVE	*E. R. Braithwaite*	75p
T041 719	HOW TO LIVE WITH A NEUROTIC DOG	*Stephen Baker*	75p
T040 925	THE PRIZE	*Irving Wallace*	£1.60
T034 755	THE CITADEL	*A. J. Cronin*	£1.10
T034 674	STRANGER IN STRANGE LAND	*Robert Heinlein*	£1.20
T037 673	BABY & CHILD CARE	*Dr Benjamin Spock*	£1.50
T037 053	79 PARK AVENUE	*Harold Robbins*	£1.25
T035 697	DUNE	*Frank Herbert*	£1.25
T035 832	THE MOON IS A HARSH MISTRESS	*Robert Heinlein*	£1.00
T040 933	THE SEVEN MINUTES	*Irving Wallace*	£1.50
T038 130	THE INHERITORS	*Harold Robbins*	£1.25
T035 689	RICH MAN POOR MAN	*Irvin Shaw*	£1.50
T037 134	EDGE 27: DEATH DRIVE	*George Gilman*	75p
T037 541	DEVIL'S GUARD	*Robert Elford*	£1.25
T038 386	THE RATS	*James Herbert*	75p
T030 342	CARRIE	*Stephen King*	75p
T033 759	THE FOG	*James Herbert*	80p
T033 740	THE MIXED BLESSING	*Helen von Slyke*	£1.25
T037 061	BLOOD AND MONEY	*Thomas Thomson*	£1.50

NEL P.O. BOX 11, FALMOUTH TR10 9EN, CORNWALL.

U.K. Customers: Please allow 22p for the first book plus 10p per copy for each additional book ordered to a maximum charge of 82p.

B.F.P.O. & Eire: Please allow 22p for the first book plus 10p per copy for the next 6 books thereafter 4p per book.

Overseas Customers: Please allow 30p for the first book plus 10p per copy for each additional book.

Name ....

Address ....

....

Title ....